celebration
CAKES

celebration CAKES

DECORATING STEP BY STEP WITH FONDANT

Grace Stevens

Contents

Introduction

I love to bake! I have been baking since I was big enough to stand on a chair and sift flour. My patient elder sister, Penny, taught me everything she knew about baking as I watched her folding, mixing and filling cakes and desserts. She instilled in me the essential respect towards the science of baking that has become the foundation on which I have built my decorating skills.

This is my first cake-decorating book and it is a dream come true to put together a collection of my cake designs to inspire other cake decorators in the same way I have been inspired by the books that fill my shelves.

You can complete each project in full or, if time does not allow, they will look just as impressive without the figures or the detailing. The modelled figures can be transferred from one project to another to create a whole new design. For instance, the fairies from the tree stump cake will look just as pretty placed on the foundation of the teddy bear cake.

It is my hope that this book will spark your imagination and, for those of you who are new to cake decorating, will help you fall hopelessly in love with the craft that has brought me so many hours of joy.

Grace Stevens

Foreword

During my years of teaching, many talented students have passed through my class. It is always exciting when you see original talent such as Grace's fresh and sometimes whimsical approach to her cakes. Her enthusiasm is infectious as she shares her techniques of modelling in easy to follow step-by-step instructions.

I recommend this book to the exhibition-minded enthusiast or to the newcomer, who from the start has the opportunity to learn this fun and easy way of making delightful novelty and children's birthday cakes. The designs can be adapted for many special occasion cakes.

Grace imparts her knowledge in a very user-friendly way as she takes you by the hand and guides you through each cake from planning stage to completion. This book deserves a place on the shelf of every cake-decorating enthusiast.

Eunice Borchers
Eunice Borchers

Equipment

The following is a list of the equipment used to create the cakes in this book:

1. round and square cutters
2. paper punch
3. calyx cutter
4. blossom cutters
5. veining tool
6. ball tool
7. bone tool
8. spirit level
9. off-set palette knife
10. serrated knife
11. sharp, non-serrated knife
12. brushes for glue and dusting
13. small 5-petal plunger cutter
14. grass tube
15. long nose pliers
16. wire cutters
17. large star tube
18. large dusting brush
19. large and small palette knives

Not photographed: large rolling pin; cake tins; Styrofoam cake dummy; turntable; filigree edge; shell tool; number 2 piping tube; scone cutter

20. guide sticks
21. carnation cutters
22. pins
23. small rolling pin
24. rose leaf plunger cutters
25. butterfly cutter
26. flower formers
27. 5-petal blossom veiners
28. daisy plunger cutters
29. cornflour bag
30. fondant smoother
31. clear, self-seal bags
32. syringe
33. toothpicks or cocktail sticks
34. nailfile or emery board

35. spatula
36. ganache/buttercream smoother
37. paper scissors
38. multi-hole extruder disks
39. ribbon extruder disks
40. roping extruder disks
41. pencil sharpener
42. nail scissors
43. tape measure
44. extruder (craft gun)
45. piping bag
46. set square
47. cel board
48. variety of straws

49

50

51

52

53

54

49. daisy centre mould
50. sponges
51. bubble impression roller
52. leaf impression mould
53. unused pot scourer
54. impression mat

55. edible glue
56. white gel colour
57. fondant
58. royal icing
59. stamens
60. CMC powder
(carboxymethyl cellulose)
61. clear piping gel
62. shortening (white margarine)
63. edible glue
64. dusting powder
65. lustre powder
66. pearl dragées
67. cake boards
68. selection of gel colour
69. florist tape
70. selection of ribbon
71. kebab stick
72. florist wire
73. wooden dowel stick
74. baking paper

55

56

57

58

59

60

61

62

63

64

65

66

67

68

69

70

71

72

73

74

Wilton
10279166
Piping Gel
Gel para decorar

Basic recipes

When beginning any cake project, it is important to begin with a sturdy and reliable base on which to decorate. I have included a few of my favourite cake recipes here. These are fantastic cakes to carve and will keep for up to a week to ensure that your cake will taste just as fantastic as it looks once you have spent two or three days putting it together.
I always use the highest-quality ingredients that I can get. This will ensure that the finished cake will 'wow' the taste buds as much as the eyes.
Always allow your cake to cool completely. Wrap the cake in clingfilm and allow it to rest for at least six hours before you use it. This allows your cake crumb to settle so that when you carve and fill your cake, it won't fall apart.

Cakes

DOUBLE CHOCOLATE CAKE *(Makes 3 x 20 cm round cakes)*

This cake freezes well for up to three months. It can be made ahead of time and allowed to defrost for an hour before it is carved and decorated.

3 jumbo eggs
100 g good-quality semi-sweet chocolate, chopped
375 ml hot coffee
2 ml vanilla bean seeds or 5 ml vanilla extract
375 ml well-shaken buttermilk
750 ml castor sugar
625 ml cake flour
375 ml unsweetened cocoa powder
10 ml bicarbonate of soda
3 ml baking powder
6 ml salt
180 ml oil

1. Preheat the oven to 150 °C. Line three 20 cm round cake tins with baking paper.
2. Beat the eggs in a mixer on high for 5–10 minutes until light and lemon coloured.
3. Mix the chocolate into the hot coffee. Allow to stand, mixing occasionally to blend.
4. Add the vanilla bean seeds or extract to the buttermilk and stir. Leave to stand.
5. Sift the sugar, flour, cocoa powder, bicarbonate of soda, baking powder and salt together in a large bowl.

6. Turn the mixer down to its lowest setting and slowly add the oil to the eggs to form an emulsion.
7. Add the buttermilk and vanilla mixture and finally the melted chocolate mixture.
8. Spoon the dry ingredients into the mixture and stir until completely combined.
9. Divide the batter between the tins and bake for 70 minutes or until a toothpick or skewer inserted into the centres comes out clean.
10. Allow to cool completely in the tins before turning the cakes out onto a wire rack, wrapping in clingfilm and allowing to settle.

HOMEMADE BUTTERMILK

Place 375 ml skim or 2% low-fat milk into a microwaveable jug and heat slightly to take off the chill. Add 60 ml lemon juice to the milk and stir. Use as you would store-bought buttermilk.

VANILLA BEAN SPONGE *(Makes 2 x 20 cm round cakes)*

When I started my cake-decorating business, I looked everywhere for the perfect vanilla bean cake. Gwenn Smith offered me her recipe and I've never used another one since. It bakes perfectly every time and can be doubled or even halved with perfect results.

3 jumbo eggs
250 ml castor sugar
250 ml milk
125 g butter, at room temperature
seeds of 1 vanilla bean or 5 ml vanilla extract
190 ml cake flour
15 ml baking powder

1. Preheat the oven to 180 °C. Line two 20 cm round cake tins with baking paper.
2. Beat the eggs and sugar in a mixer on high for at least 10 minutes until light and fluffy.
3. Heat the milk, butter and vanilla bean seeds or extract in a saucepan until the butter melts.
4. Sift the flour and baking powder into a bowl at least three times to incorporate air.
5. Turn down the mixer to low and, beginning and ending with the flour, pour the milk mixture slowly into the bowl while spooning the flour in one tablespoon at a time. Do this part as quickly as possible to avoid over-mixing your batter.
6. Divide the batter between the tins and bake for 22 minutes or until a toothpick or skewer inserted into the centres comes out clean.
7. Turn the cakes out of the tins and cool on a wire rack for 5 minutes before wrapping in clingfilm.

COCONUT SPONGE *(Makes 2 x 20 cm round cakes)*

This light sponge has a delicate taste of coconut that is perfect paired with lemon-mascarpone buttercream.

60 ml desiccated coconut
3 jumbo eggs
250 ml castor sugar
250 ml coconut cream
125 g butter, at room temperature
375 ml cake flour
15 ml baking powder

1. Preheat the oven to 180 °C. Line two 20 cm round cake tins with baking paper.
2. Toast the coconut in a dry pan until lightly toasted.
3. Beat the eggs and sugar in a mixer on high for at least 10 minutes until light and fluffy.
4. Heat the coconut cream and butter in a saucepan until the butter melts.
5. Sift the flour and baking powder into a bowl at least three times to incorporate air before adding the toasted coconut.
6. Turn down the mixer to low and, beginning and ending with the flour, pour the coconut cream mixture slowly into the bowl while spooning the flour in one tablespoon at a time. Do this part as quickly as possible to avoid over-mixing your batter.
7. Divide the batter between the tins and bake for 22 minutes or until a toothpick or skewer inserted into the centres comes out clean.
8. Turn the cakes out of the tins and cool on a wire rack for 5 minutes before wrapping in clingfilm.

CARROT CAKE *(Makes 3 x 20 cm round cakes)*

4 eggs
375 ml brown sugar
250 ml cooking oil
500 ml cake flour
10 ml baking powder
3 ml salt
5 ml ground cinnamon
3 ml ground ginger
3 ml ground cloves
3 ml mixed spice
2 ml bicarbonate of soda
700 ml finely grated carrots
125 ml finely grated apple
125 ml seedless raisins (optional)
125 ml chopped walnuts

1. Preheat the oven to 180 °C. Line two 20 cm round cake tins or three 15 cm round cake tins with baking paper.
2. Whisk the eggs and sugar together until light and fluffy. Add the oil and mix well.
3. Sift the dry ingredients together and add to the egg mixture. Use a metal spoon to fold in the carrots, apple, raisins and walnuts. Stir lightly to blend well.
4. Divide the batter between the tins and bake for 35 minutes or until a toothpick or skewer inserted into the centres comes out clean. Cool the cakes in the tins for five minutes and then turn out and cool on a wire rack.

> TIP: You can choose to leave out the raisins in this recipe, as they will make sculpting a cake difficult. This cake is best served with lemon- or orange-mascarpone buttercream.

Fillings

Layers between cakes can be filled with a variety of tasty fillings. When a cake is to be carved, the filling needs to be stable enough to hold the shape of the cake and not allow the layers to slide around while you are carving it. After filling and layering a cake, allow the filling to settle and firm up before carving or covering the cake with ganache.

I make buttercream in a food processor. This method ensures that the buttercream is always smooth and that not too much air is incorporated into the filling. You can use a mixer with a paddle attachment to make this with similar results.

VANILLA BUTTERCREAM (*Makes enough to fill one 20 cm round or square cake*)

100 g butter
100 g good-quality white margarine
500 g icing sugar
seeds of ½ vanilla bean or 5 ml vanilla extract
approximately 35 ml milk

1. Cream the butter, margarine and icing sugar in a bowl.
2. Add the vanilla bean seeds or extract and slowly add the milk until the desired consistency is achieved. The buttercream should hold its shape, but not be too stiff. If it's too stiff, add 5 ml milk at a time until the buttercream can be spread without pulling the crumbs off the cake.
3. Cover the bowl with clingfilm until needed. Refrigerate overnight and allow to stand out for an hour before using to fill a cake.

VARIATIONS
COFFEE BUTTERCREAM: Substitute chilled coffee for the milk.
CHOCOLATE BUTTERCREAM: Add 45 ml cocoa powder and 30 ml chilled coffee.
LEMON OR ORANGE BUTTERCREAM: Add the zest of ½ lemon or orange and substitute freshly squeezed lemon or orange juice for the milk.

MASCARPONE BUTTERCREAM *(Makes enough to fill one 20 cm round or square cake)*

This is a rich cream cheese buttercream that is perfect for a cake to be used as a dessert.

75 g mascarpone cheese
50 g butter
75 g full-cream cream cheese
500 g icing sugar
seeds of ½ vanilla bean or 5 ml vanilla extract

1. Cream the mascarpone, butter, cream cheese and icing sugar in a bowl until a firm buttercream forms.
2. Add the vanilla bean seeds or extract. If the buttercream is too firm for filling a cake, beat in 15 ml milk at a time until the consistency is correct.
3. Cover the bowl with clingfilm and store in the fridge until needed. This will keep for up to a week.

VARIATIONS

COFFEE-MASCARPONE BUTTERCREAM: Substitute 25 ml chilled coffee for the vanilla.
CHOCOLATE-MASCARPONE BUTTERCREAM: Add 30 ml cocoa powder and 30 ml chilled coffee.
LEMON- OR ORANGE-MASCARPONE BUTTERCREAM: Add the zest and juice of ½ lemon or orange.

LAVENDER BUTTERCREAM *(Makes enough to fill one 20 cm round or square cake)*

125 ml castor sugar
125 ml water
3 organic lavender flowers/stalks (washed)
1 quantity mascarpone or vanilla buttercream

LAVENDER SYRUP

1. Place the sugar and water in a saucepan over a high heat and bring to the boil (do not stir). Boil for 2 minutes to make the syrup.
2. Remove the syrup from the heat and decant into a heatproof bowl.
3. Infuse the syrup with the lavender by gently placing the flowers into the syrup.
4. Leave the lavender in the syrup for 15 minutes (any longer and the syrup will become bitter).
5. Remove the lavender and pour the syrup into a screw-top jar. Store in the fridge for up to two weeks.

TO MAKE THE BUTTERCREAM
Add between 3–8 ml of lavender syrup to the buttercream and blend well.

TIP: This buttercream complements the double chocolate cake perfectly and creates a truly special twist when used to fill a vanilla bean sponge.

Coverings

Ganache is a combination of chocolate and cream that can be used to both fill and cover cakes. It sets very firm once it has stood for a few hours. Covering a cake in ganache provides an excellent base on which to cover a cake in fondant.

DARK CHOCOLATE GANACHE *(Makes enough to cover one 20 cm round or square cake)*

250 ml double-thick cream
500 g good-quality dark chocolate, roughly chopped

1. Heat the cream on a low heat until small bubbles form on the edges of the saucepan (just before boiling).
2. Remove the pan from the heat, add the chocolate and stir until all the chocolate melts.
3. Allow the ganache to cool until it is the consistency of soft buttercream.
4. Store in the fridge overnight and soften by placing the ganache in a microwaveable bowl and heating it for 10 seconds at a time until the correct consistency is achieved.

WHITE CHOCOLATE GANACHE *(Makes enough to cover one 20 cm round or square cake)*

White ganache is perfect for covering vanilla bean, carrot and red velvet cakes as the taste does not compete with the distinctive flavours of these cakes.

250 ml double-thick cream
750 g good-quality white chocolate, roughly chopped

1. Heat the cream on a low heat until small bubbles form on the edges of the saucepan (just before boiling).
2. Remove the pan from the heat, add the chocolate and stir until all the chocolate melts.
3. Allow the ganache to cool until it is the consistency of soft buttercream.
4. Store in the fridge overnight and soften by placing the ganache in a microwaveable bowl and heating it for 10 seconds at a time until the correct consistency is achieved.

MODELLING PASTE *(Makes 500 g)*

5–10 ml CMC (carboxymethyl cellulose) powder
500 g fondant

1. Knead the CMC powder into the fondant.
2. Store in a self-sealing bag or wrap in clingfilm to prevent it from drying out.

FLOWER PASTE *(Makes 480 g)*

white shortening
500 ml sifted icing sugar
12 ml tylose powder
11 ml tap water
5 ml gelatine
1 egg white

1. Grease a 1-litre glass bowl with shortening. Add half of the icing sugar and the tylose powder. Mix well with your fingertips.
2. Microwave for about 2 minutes, checking and mixing with your fingertips after each 30 seconds. Set aside.
3. Place the tap water in a clean, small glass bowl and sprinkle over the gelatine. It is important that the gelatine goes on top of the water. Microwave this for 24 seconds, checking after each 6 seconds that the gelatine is dissolving and not 'stringy'.
4. Remove from the microwave and add the egg white. Beat until well combined – it does not have to be stiff. Pour this into the icing sugar and tylose mixture and blend with an electric mixer, gradually adding the remaining icing sugar.
5. Once the mixture is too thick to use the mixer, turn out onto a clean surface and knead into a soft ball. The end product should not be sticky and if it is, add a little more sifted icing sugar until a good soft dough is achieved. Rub a bean-sized amount of shortening onto your hands and mix this into the paste thoroughly.
6. Wrap in clingfilm and place in a clean jar with a lid that seals tightly. Refrigerate overnight. Use the following day and ensure that you keep the paste well-wrapped in clingfilm and in the sealed jar at all times to prevent drying out. The paste is best stored in the fridge.

EDIBLE GLUE *(Makes 50 ml)*

This glue is brushed on with a small dry brush. It keeps well for weeks.

2 ml CMC (carboxymethyl cellulose) powder
50 ml warm water

1. Add the CMC powder to the warm water.
2. Cover and allow to stand overnight. If the glue is too thick, thin it down with 5 ml warm water.
3. Store in a container with a screw-top lid to prevent the glue from drying out.

ROYAL ICING *(Makes 125 ml)*

Royal icing is fairly quick-setting and becomes very hard once it has set. It is fantastic for icing delicate work and can be very useful when attaching figures to cakes.

1 egg white
250 ml icing sugar, finely sifted

1. Beat the egg white until foamy with a wooden spoon or small whisk.
2. Slowly add the icing sugar, one tablespoon at a time, whisking continuously.
3. Continue beating until stiff peaks form. (A stiff peak should form when the whisk or wooden spoon is pulled out of the icing.)
4. Cover with clingfilm and refrigerate until needed. The icing will need to be whisked up once it has stood for a few hours.

TIP: If royal icing is too stiff, dilute with a small amount of egg white, mixing well until the icing is the desired consistency.

Techniques

There are many techniques used by decorators to achieve a specific look for a celebration cake. Approaching a cake project can be quite intimidating, especially if it includes some techniques that you are not familiar with or that you have not yet mastered. In this chapter, I have grouped together the techniques that are used repeatedly throughout the cake projects. You can refer back to this section while completing these projects or use this chapter as a place to practise these techniques and hone your skills.

FILLING A CAKE

Use cooled cake layers that have rested for at least 6 hours.

1. Level the layers with a sharp serrated knife.
2. Place the first layer onto a cake board and with a large palette knife, drop a large portion of filling (buttercream or ganache) in the centre of the cake. Smooth out the filling from the centre towards the edges. Add more filling if required. The palette knife should not touch the cake.
3. Stack the cake with a second levelled layer, and press down gently to make sure that the cakes stick to the filling. Repeat to add a third layer, etc.

SCULPTING A CAKE

1. Level, fill and stack the cake layers. Set aside to allow the filling to settle.
2. With a serrated knife, remove small amounts of cake a little at a time until
    the cake is the desired shape.

SCULPTING A SQUARE TOPSY-TURVY CAKE

A square topsy-turvy or wonky cake is narrower at the base of the cake than at the top. Often the top of the cake is also carved to a slant, so that the left side of the cake is higher than the right side. This cake often needs an extra layer to emphasise the shape and height. To carve this shape, it is important to have a well-rested cake, at least 6 hours after it has cooled. The cake will be carved upside-down and then turned over to be covered in fondant and decorated (illustrated overleaf).

1. Level each cake layer and fill and stack the layers. Allow the filled cake to rest for at least
    half an hour.
2. For a 20 cm square cake, position a 15 cm square cake board in the centre of the top
    of the cake.
3. Using a serrated knife, cut from the edge of the 15 cm square diagonally down and
    out to the base of the cake. Rotate the cake and cut each side in the same way.
4. Flip the cake so that the base becomes the top.
5. Cut a wedge off the top of the cake to create a slanting top.

GANACHING A CAKE

1. Level, fill and stack the cake layers. At this stage, the cake can be sculpted.
2. With a large, off-set palette knife, place a small amount of ganache on the top and smooth it from the top of the cake over and around the edges.
3. Add ganache a little at a time as needed. The palette knife should not touch the cake. If the ganache pulls crumbs off the cake, clean the palette knife or heat the ganache slightly.
4. When the cake is completely covered in ganache, run a clean palette knife over the ganache until the surface of the cake is smooth. Clean the palette knife regularly to achieve a smooth result.

COVERING A CAKE

1. Level, fill, stack and ganache the cake. Allow the ganache to set firm before covering in fondant.
2. On a well cornflour-dusted surface, roll out fondant to a thickness of 3 mm.
3. Brush the outside of the ganached cake with clear alcohol or lemon juice.
4. Lift the rolled-out fondant and gently lower it onto the cake.
5. With the palms of your hands, smooth the fondant onto the cake from the top to the base. Flare the fondant gently away from the base to avoid creasing.
6. Trim excess fondant with a sharp knife.
7. Use a small ball of excess fondant to smooth over the surface of the cake.

DOWELLING A CAKE

Dowelling is when multiple covered cakes are stacked. The upper cake in each instance is supported by dowels, so that it appears to be resting on the cake below. This is just an illusion.

1. Before dowelling can take place, the cakes and cake boards must be prepared and covered with fondant.
2. Measure the depth of the bottom cake by inserting a kebab stick vertically through the centre of the cake. Mark the stick about 2 mm above the top of the fondant.
3. Remove the stick and use the measurement to cut five dowels to that length.
4. Rest the empty cake tin in which the upper cake was baked on top of the bottom cake. Make sure that it is in the exact position that the upper cake will be placed. Use the tin as a guide and mark out the perimeter of the tin with a pin tip. When the empty cake tin is removed, it will be easy to see where the upper cake should be placed on the bottom cake.
5. Clean the dowels with clear alcohol or lemon juice before inserting them into the bottom cake within the shape marked out with the pin. Ensure that the dowels are evenly spaced.
6. Place the upper cake on a cake board, then place both over the dowels, using a small amount of ganache or royal icing to secure it.

COVERING A CAKE BOARD

Covering a cake board will add a more finished and professional look to a cake.
It is quick and easy to do.

1. Dust the work surface well with cornflour, then roll out enough fondant to cover the board.
2. Brush the top surface of the board with a little water or edible glue.
3. Drape the rolled-out fondant over the board and smooth out with a smoother. At this stage, an impression mat or impression roller can be pushed into the fondant to create a textured surface.
4. Trim the edges with a sharp knife to keep the shape of the board.
5. Choose a matching ribbon for the cake design and cut the ribbon to fit the circumference of the board. Stick the ribbon around the edge with non-toxic glue.

COLOURING FONDANT AND MODELLING PASTE

Use a good-quality gel colour to colour fondant and modelling paste – liquid colours will make fondant sticky.

1. Dip a toothpick into the gel colour and touch it to the fondant or modelling paste.
2. Knead in the colour until it is completely mixed. Add more colour if a more vibrant colour is required. Remember that it is easier to build up a colour than to tone it down, so add colour slowly.
3. If a unique colour is to be created using two different colours, first mix the lighter colour, then add the darker one until the desired colour is achieved.

FONDANT SAND

A wonderfully generous member of the Icing Guild showed us how to make this.
I have added lustre dust and glitter to the recipe for a more magical touch.

1. Roll out brown fondant to a thickness of 1 mm. Allow the fondant to dry out overnight.
2. With a sharp knife, chop the fondant into fine, sand grain–like pieces. Place these pieces into a clear bag.
3. Add half a teaspoon of brown lustre dust and half a teaspoon of brown glitter. Shake the bag to mix. This will keep well in a sealed bottle.

BLOSSOMS

Although it is best to make blossoms ahead of time, they can be made and used immediately. Take care with wet blossoms as they are more fragile than when they are dry.

1. Roll out white flower paste to a thickness of 2 mm.
2. With a blossom cutter, cut out a blossom shape.
3. Place the blossom into a five-petal blossom veiner and gently press the two parts of the veiner together.
4. Remove the veined blossom from the mould and allow to dry before dusting the centre with petal dust.
5. Glue a single sugar dragée into the centre of the blossom with edible glue.

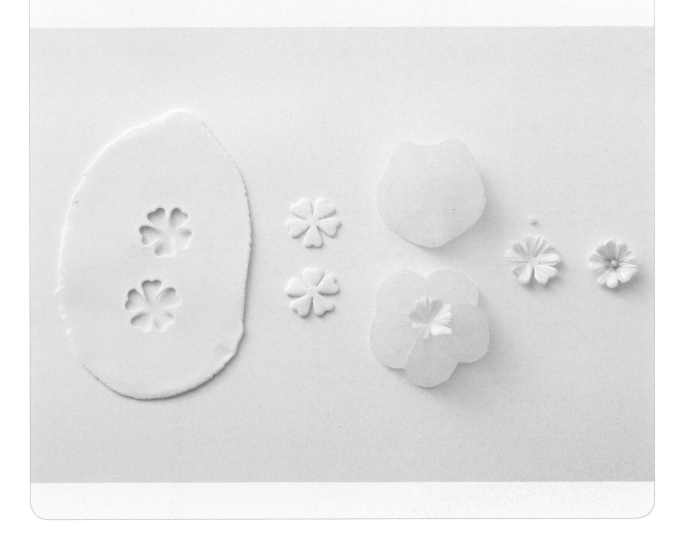

FACES

1. Colour modelling paste in a flesh tone. Roll a smooth ball in the palm of your hand.
2. Mould a wide calabash shape, narrower at one end. The narrower end will become the top of the head. Pinch along the centre to create cheek bones.
3. With a small circle cutter, imprint a semi-circle into the lower half of the face beginning just under the cheeks. Open the mouth with the large point of a veining tool.
4. Roll a tiny ball of paste for a nose and attach with edible glue.
5. Roll two tiny black balls of paste for eyes and attach with edible glue.
6. Brush the mouth and cheeks with pink petal dust.
7. Mark the glint in each eye by dipping the tip of a toothpick into some white gel colour and dotting it onto the top left-hand side of each eye.
8. Adding hair will change the face into a girl or a boy. Rounder faces are used for babies and children. Elongate the face for older characters.

HAIR

1. Mix two colours of modelling paste for the hair, one slightly lighter than the other.
2. Knead a little shortening into the paste to make it more fluid.
3. Roll the two colours into a ball, marbling the colour rather than completely mixing them. When these colours are extruded from the craft gun, they will create a natural hair colour.
4. Cover the back of the figure's head with edible glue.
5. Extrude lengths of paste from the craft gun using the multi-holed disk. These will look like strands of hair.
6. Attach the hair to the nape of the neck, covering the base of the head. Repeat, adding a second row on top of the first, but slightly higher up on the head. Add a third row and turn the figure to face you.
7. Extrude two shorter pieces of paste and place on either side of the forehead to create a fringe.

ARMS

1. Colour modelling paste in a flesh tone. Divide the required amount of paste into two balls.
2. With the first ball, roll a sausage shape with a small bulb at one end.
3. Halfway along the sausage shape, bend the paste between your thumb and forefinger to create an elbow. Shape the elbow into a sharp bend and with the back of a knife score creases into the inside of the elbow.
4. Gently flatten the bulb shape by pushing it flat on a work surface.
5. Cut a thumb and four fingers with a sharp knife. Shape the fingers between your own fingers and shape the hand to fit with the model's pose.
6. Repeat with the second ball to make the other arm. Take care to make the thumbs on each hand closest to the model's body.

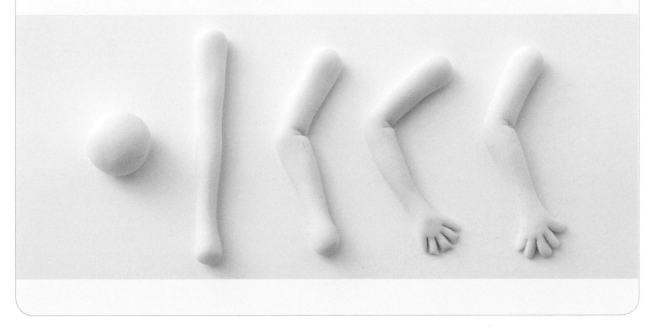

LEGS

1. Colour modelling paste in a flesh tone. Divide the required amount of paste into two balls.
2. With the first ball, roll a sausage shape with a small bulb at one end.
3. Halfway along the sausage shape, pinch the paste between your thumb and forefinger to create a knee. Shape the knee to make a strong angle. Score creases into the back of the knee using, the back of a knife.
4. Flatten the bulb at the end on a work surface to make a foot.
5. Place a finger under the foot and pinch the heel with your thumb. Shape the foot with your fingers, narrowing it and shaping the toes until it is the desired shape.
6. Repeat with the second ball to make the other leg.

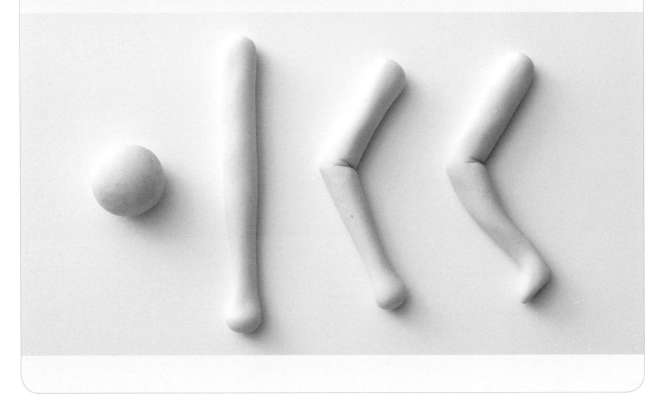

FAIRY WINGS

Unbreakable lace, as taught to me by the incredibly talented Eunice Borchers, is the perfect medium for creating transparent and delicate fairy wings.

1. Mix 5 ml CMC powder with 50 ml warm water. Cover and leave overnight to dissolve.
2. Mix a little gel colour into the mixture the next day.
3. Spread this gummy mixture onto a flat surface such as a tile or a piece of clear plastic, taking care not to spread it too thin.

4. Dip a dry brush into some edible glitter and tap the brush over the wet paste to add sparkle to the wings.

5. Allow the paste to dry overnight. It will shrink considerably and will become very thin and appear brittle. Slide an off-set palette knife carefully under the dried paste to remove it from the tile or plastic.

6. Trace the fairy princess wings template on page 143 onto a sheet of baking paper and carefully cut them out.

7. Fold the unbreakable lace (dried paste) in half. Fold the cut-out of the fairy wings down the centre and slot the paper between the folded unbreakable lace. Use a sharp pair of scissors to cut out the wings using the template cut-out as a guide.

8. Attach the wings to the fairy's back with a dot of royal icing. Unbreakable lace will keep indefinitely if kept away from moisture.

Baby in a teacup cake

This delicate cake can grace the table at a baby shower, christening or even a first birthday.
Substitute the tiny teddy bear for a favourite toy if you wish.

Recipes

- 1 quantity double chocolate cake baked in three 20 cm round cake tins (p. 18)
- 1 quantity chocolate buttercream (variations p. 21)
- 1 quantity dark chocolate ganache (p. 23)
- 1 quantity royal icing (p. 25)

EQUIPMENT

impression mat

teacup and saucer

cornflour bag for dusting

small and large rolling pins

templates for teacup and handle (p. 145)

baking paper

sharp knife

pair of scissors

primula blossom cutter

sharp dowel

edge cutters

small heart plunger cutter

lace

medium carnation cutter

toothpicks

straw

veining tool

small paintbrush

extruder

bone tool

plastic clingfilm

medium calyx cutter

medium rose leaf plunger cutter

nail file

large soft paintbrush

small syringe

fondant smoother

MATERIALS

35 cm round cake board

ribbon

900 g ivory fondant

310 g ivory modelling paste

60 g flesh-toned modelling paste

50 g flame-red modelling paste

40 g dark pink modelling paste

30 g black modelling paste

20 g white modelling paste

20 g red modelling paste

20 g light pink modelling paste

20 g coral modelling paste

14 g dark brown modelling paste

70 g moss-green flower paste

50 g flame-red flower paste

50 g dark pink flower paste

50 g coral flower paste

50 g light pink flower paste

clear alcohol or lemon juice

clear piping gel

cornflour

non-toxic glue

edible glue

ivory gel colour

powder pink lustre dust

petal dust

shortening

support stick

20 white stamens

Preparation

THREE DAYS OR UP TO A WEEK IN ADVANCE:
Make the baby in a teacup topper over two days, allowing at least 8 hours for the teacup
and saucer to dry before adding the blankets, baby and teddy.

TWO DAYS IN ADVANCE:
Make 45 free-form roses from flame-red, coral and dark pink flower paste.
Make 30 rose leaves from moss-green flower paste.
Make 10 light pink flowers.
Bake the cake layers, and allow to cool and settle.
Cover the cake board in 550 g ivory fondant, emboss with an impression mat and glue
the ribbon around the edge with non-toxic glue.

ONE DAY IN ADVANCE:
Fill and stack the cake layers.

Cover the cake in chocolate ganache and allow to set.

TEACUP

1. Mix a pea-sized amount of shortening into the ivory modelling paste. This will delay the drying-out of the paste, allowing more time for modelling the teacup and saucer.

2. Dust the inside and outside of a teacup with a generous amount of cornflour. This will prevent the paste from sticking to the cup. Turn the teacup upside-down on the work surface.

3. Evenly roll out 150 g ivory modelling paste to 2 mm thick. Trace the teacup template on page 145 onto baking paper and cut out the shape. Lay the template on top of the rolled-out paste and carefully cut around it with a sharp knife. Spread edible glue along one straight edge and overlap to make a paste cone.

4. Drape the cone over the inverted teacup and gently shape it over the cup with your fingers. This will prepare the shape for the inside of the teacup.

5. When the paste has taken on a dome shape, turn over the cup, remove the paste from the outside and place it inside. With your fingertips, work the paste until it is smooth and has taken on the shape of the teacup.

6. Trim the excess paste on the rim of the cup with a sharp knife or a pair of scissors. Make sure that the paste does not stick to the rim of the cup. Allow to dry in the cup for about 10 minutes.

7. Remove the paste from the cup and dust the inside of the cup with more cornflour. Return the paste to the cup to dry for a few more hours.

8. Remove the paste teacup from the real teacup and allow to dry overnight. Keep the paste cup away from moisture and extreme temperatures.

SAUCER

1—4

1. Roll out 100 g ivory modelling paste to 2 mm thick.

2. Dust a saucer with cornflour.

3. Drape the rolled-out paste over the saucer and gently work it into the grooves with your fingertips.

4. Trim the edges of the paste along the edge of the saucer with a sharp knife. Check to see that the paste is not stuck to the saucer by gently rotating it in the saucer. Allow to dry overnight.

TEACUP HANDLE

1. Trace the teacup-handle template on page 145 onto baking paper.
2. Roll 20 g ivory modelling paste into a smooth ball.
3. Roll the ball into a sausage 7 mm wide.
4. Use the template to create the shape of the handle. Allow to dry on the paper overnight.
5. Attach the handle to the seam of the dried teacup with a few dots of royal icing.

BLANKETS AND PILLOW

1. Place a large golf ball sized ball (30–40 g) of ivory modelling paste inside the dry modelled teacup, attaching it to the bottom with some edible glue. This will form the base onto which the blankets and pillows will be placed.
2. Roll out 20 g red, 20 g light pink, 20 g dark pink and 20 g coral modelling paste to a thickness of 1 mm.
3. Cut out blankets 7 x 8 cm with a sharp knife.
4. Shape a pillow from 20 g dark pink modelling paste. Create fabric patterns on the blankets and pillow with impression mats, lace, blossom cutters and edge cutters.
5. Drape the blankets over the edge of the teacup to create a bed and place the pillow on the rim of the teacup opposite the cup handle.

BABY BODY

1. Shape 20 g flesh-toned modelling paste into a teardrop to form the body of the baby.
2. Glue the body on top of the blankets with edible glue. The wide end of the teardrop must be closest to the cup handle. The narrow end will become the baby's shoulders.
3. Divide 15 g flesh-toned modelling paste into four balls to create arms and legs using the techniques on page 35 and 36. Bend the legs at the knee and the arms at the elbow and tuck them under the body, as if she is sleeping on her stomach.

BABY DRESS

1—4

1. Roll out 20 g white modelling paste to a thickness of 2 mm. Cut out two carnation blossoms with a medium carnation cutter, as well as one smaller blossom.
2. Cut the blossoms in half with a sharp knife.
3. Frill each blossom with the end of a toothpick.
4. Attach the frilled carnations to the wide end of the body to create a layered, frilly skirt. The skirt should go up to the waist of the body and cover the baby's bottom. Cut and frill extra carnations if you prefer a fuller skirt.
5. Attach the smaller frilled blossom to the narrow end of the body to create a collar, making sure to cover the joins where the arms are attached.

RIBBON

1. Roll out 20 g flame-red modelling paste and cut out three ribbons: two rectangles 15 x 8 mm and one 10 x 8 mm.
2. Pinch each end of the longer ribbons as shown.
3. Fold them over to create a loop.
4. Glue the pinched ends together with edible glue.
5. Roll the shorter ribbon with a rolling pin until it is twice as wide and very thin.
6. Pinch the two ends together to create a pleated ribbon as shown.
7. Wrap this ribbon around the centre of the joined loops.
8. Secure underneath with edible glue.
9. Glue the ribbon to the back of the baby's dress.

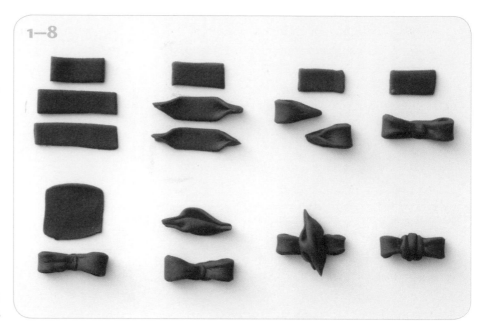

BABY FACE

1. Roll 15 g flesh-toned modelling paste into a smooth ball. Roll a proportionately smaller ball also from flesh-toned paste.
2. Shape the larger ball into a calabash.
3. Press the top of a straw into the paste to create two closed eyelids and tiny eyelashes.
4. Divide the smaller ball of paste into two balls for ears and a smaller one for a nose.

5. Create a mouth with a veining tool by pushing the wider end into the paste and rocking it side to side to open the mouth.

6. Push the end of a small paintbrush into the two small balls to create the ears. Glue the ears to the sides of the face and the nose on the front.

7. Push 20 g black modelling paste through an extruder to create tiny strands of hair. Attach the hair to the head with edible glue.

8. Dip a toothpick in ivory gel colour and paint on eyebrows and tiny freckles to add detail to the face.

TINY TEDDY

1. Roll two smooth balls from 5 g and 3 g dark brown modelling paste.

2. Shape the larger into a teardrop for the body.

3. Mark the bear's belly button with a toothpick. Divide the smaller ball into four for the limbs.

4. Shape each into a tiny, slightly curved teardrop.

5. Attach the limbs to the body with edible glue.

6. Roll two smooth balls from 4 g and 2 g dark brown modelling paste.

7. Shape the larger into a teardrop for the head. Fold the narrow end up to create a muzzle.

8. Divide the smaller ball into two for the ears.

9. Shape each into tiny teardrops and press the small end of a bone tool into the wider end of each to create the ears.

10. Mark the position of the eyes with a toothpick and form the mouth by pushing the end of a veining tool into the paste below the muzzle. Push the back of a knife down the centre of the muzzle.

11. Attach the ears to the head with edible glue.

12. Roll two tiny balls of black modelling paste and glue them over the eye markings with edible glue. Dip a toothpick in ivory gel paint and paint a glint in each eye.

13. Roll and squash a small ball of black modelling paste into an oval. Glue this to the bear's muzzle with edible glue.

14. Insert a stick into the body between the shoulders to support the head. Position the body in the teacup before attaching the head. Thread the head onto the support stick and secure with edible glue.

ROSES

1. Roll a grape-sized piece of coral flower paste into a ball.
2. Flatten the ball between two sheets of plastic.
3. Use the nail on your forefinger to press and thin the top part into a petal shape. Keep the bottom part thick.
4. Remove the petal from the plastic.
5. Roll into a cone shape as shown. This will form the base of the rose.
6. Work two more balls of paste between the plastic. Wrap the thin edge of one petal around the base of the cone. Tuck the second petal under the first and wrap tightly around the bud.
7. Gently fan out the petals to open the rose. Add more petals to make a bigger rose. Tuck each petal under the one before.
8. Pinch the bottom of the rose to remove any excess paste and to form a neat and rounded base for the flower.
9. Roll out 20 g moss-green flower paste to about 1 mm thick. Cut out a calyx.

10. Attach to the underside of the rose with edible glue once the rose has dried.
11. Dust the rose with petal dust to highlight each petal.
12. If you would like to add a stem, wrap the desired length of florist wire in green florist tape and insert into the rose before it dries. Attach rose leaves with dots of edible glue.

ROSE LEAVES

1. Roll 50 g moss-green flower paste into a smooth ball.
2. Roll out to a thickness of 1 mm.
3. Cut out 30 rose leaves with a medium rose leaf plunger cutter.
4. Shape each leaf before drying.

LIGHT PINK FLOWERS

1. Roll 5 g light pink flower paste into a ball.
2. Form the ball into a cone and pinch the wider side flat, leaving a narrow stalk.
3. Place the flattened cone onto the work surface, flat-side down.
4. Place a small primula cutter over the stalk and cut out the blossom shape.
5. Hollow out the centre of the flat side with a sharpened dowel to create a trumpet-shaped flower.
6. Dust the hollow of the flower with powder pink lustre dust.
7. Insert two white stamens into the hollow of the flower to finish.

ASSEMBLING THE CUP AND SAUCER

1. Smooth the edges of the paste saucer by gently filing them with a clean nail file. Remove paste dust with a large, clean paintbrush.
2. Attach the teacup to the saucer with edible glue or a small dot of royal icing.
3. Rest a single rose in the saucer and glue in place with edible glue.
4. Draw 2 ml clear piping gel into a small syringe and push a tiny drop of gel onto the outside of one rose petal. This will dry to look like a dewdrop.

ASSEMBLY

1. Roll out 900 g ivory fondant to a thickness of 2 mm.
2. Brush the surface of the ganached cake with clear alcohol or lemon juice.
3. Cover the ganache with the rolled-out fondant, smoothing the surface with a fondant smoother. Trim excess fondant and transfer the cake to the prepared cake board.
4. Attach the roses to the bottom edge of the cake with dots of royal icing. Fill the gaps with rose leaves and light pink flowers, attaching them in the same way.
5. Push a small drop of clear piping gel onto one petal of each rose for dewdrops.
6. Position the teacup on top of the cake, using royal icing to hold it in place.

Quilted daisy cake

Daisies have a wonderfully cheerful quality about them. They are whimsical and innocent. I first made this cake as a single tier for my best friend's birthday a few years ago. This version is a little more sophisticated and would suit a garden party perfectly.

Recipes

- 1½ quantities double chocolate cake baked in three 20 cm round cake tins and three 15 cm round cake tins (p. 18)
- 1 quantity chocolate buttercream (variations p. 21)
- 2 quantities dark chocolate ganache (p. 23)
- 1 quantity royal icing (p. 25)

EQUIPMENT
large and small rolling pins
impression mat
large and small daisy cutters
flower shaper
daisy centre impression mould
scouring pad
small paintbrush
small daisy plunger cutter
baking paper
toothpicks
palette knife
veining tool
dowel
piping bag
medium rose leaf plunger cutter
pair of scissors
small-holed disk extruder

MATERIALS
35 cm round cake board
ribbon
2 kg white fondant
180 g white flower paste
50 g egg-yellow flower paste
50 g moss-green flower paste
25 g moss-green modelling paste
shortening
non-toxic glue
edible glue
buttercup-yellow petal dust
96 yellow dragées

Preparation

UP TO A WEEK IN ADVANCE:
Make 5 large daisies and 96 small daisies, plus a few extra in case of breakage.
Make 11 rose leaves using the technique on page 46.
Cover the cake board with 550 g white fondant rolled to a thickness of 2 mm. Smooth the surface of the fondant before pressing an impression mat onto the surface.
Glue the ribbon around the edge of the cake board with non-toxic glue.

TWO DAYS IN ADVANCE:
Bake the cake layers, and allow to cool and settle.

ONE DAY IN ADVANCE:
Level and fill the cakes, making one 20 cm cake with three layers and one 15 cm cake with three layers.
Cover both cakes in dark chocolate ganache.

LARGE DAISIES

1. Roll out 100 g white flower paste to a thickness of 1 mm.
2. Cut out one large and one small daisy with daisy cutters. Place each cut-out daisy in a flower shaper to dry. Flower paste is a lot more fragile while it is drying, so make sure the flowers are not moved until they are completely dry.
3. Roll 8 g egg-yellow flower paste into a smooth ball. Press one side of the ball into a daisy centre impression mould or roll the ball on a clean scouring pad.
4. When the daisies are dry, glue the smaller one onto the larger one with a little edible glue and glue the flattened ball into the centre.
5. Dust the centre with buttercup-yellow petal dust, dusting halfway up each petal.

6. Make five daisies and a few extra in case of breakage.

SMALL DAISIES

1. Roll out 80 g white flower paste to a thickness of 1 mm.
2. Cut out daisies with a small daisy plunger cutter.
3. Dust each centre with buttercup-yellow petal dust.
4. Glue a yellow dragée in the centre of each flower.
5. Make 96 small daisies and a few extra in case of breakage. Allow to dry.

TENDRILS

1. Mix a small amount of shortening with 25 g moss-green modelling paste.
2. Place the paste into an extruder. Extrude 12 cm lengths of paste through a small-holed disk extruder.
3. Wrap each length of paste around a toothpick and allow to set for about 5–10 minutes. Carefully remove the tendrils of paste from the toothpicks; they will hold their shape (see page 57).

QUILT

1. Brush the ganached cakes with clear alcohol or lemon juice.
2. Roll out the remaining white fondant and use to individually cover the cakes.
3. Cut out a 15 cm circle of baking paper. Fold the circle in half, then into quarters and finally into eighths. Open the circle and the shape will be divided into eight equal wedges.
4. Lay the circle of baking paper on top of the 15 cm cake. It is important to do this while the fondant is still soft. Use a toothpick to mark where each fold in the paper meets at the edge of the cake. At the base of the cake, use a toothpick to mark directly under the top marking.
5. To mark the quilt, one dot from the top row of dots is joined to a dot on the bottom row with a straight line. Using the flat side of a palette knife to make each line, join the dot on the top row with the dot to the right on the bottom row. Continue around the cake until all the dots are joined with a straight line. Repeat these markings from the opposite direction, joining the top dot to one below and to the left of it.
6. Mark where each line crosses with the small side of a veining tool.

7. Attach a small daisy to each cross point with a tiny dot of royal icing.
8. Repeat with the 20 cm cake, using a 20 cm circle of baking paper.

ASSEMBLY

1. Place the 20 cm cake onto the prepared cake board.
2. Dowel the bottom cake and stack the 15 cm one in the centre of it.
3. Pipe a small border of royal icing around the base of each cake.
4. Attach the large daisies with edible glue and add a few rose leaves and tendrils to fill in the gaps and finish it off.

Tree stump cake

When I was a little girl, I slept with my *Flower Fairies* picture book under my pillow. This cake brings some of those pages to life. If you are short on time, a tree stump without fairies is equally enchanting.

Recipes

- 1 quantity vanilla bean sponge baked in three 15 cm round cake tins (p. 19)
- 1 quantity royal icing (p. 25)
- 1 quantity lemon-mascarpone buttercream (variations p. 22)
- 1 quantity white chocolate ganache (p. 23)

EQUIPMENT

large and small rolling pins
bubble impression roller
sharp knife
fondant smoother
veining tool
large dusting brush
butterfly paper punch
toothpicks
large and small paintbrushes
Styrofoam cake dummy
medium five-petal blossom cutter
five-petal blossom veiner
template for fairy wings (p. 143)
baking paper
small-holed disk extruder
medium carnation cutter
icing bag
grass tube
primula blossom cutter
small blossom cutter

MATERIALS

30 cm round cake board
ribbon
550 g moss-green fondant
400 g light brown fondant
400 g dark brown fondant
120 g white modelling paste
120 g flesh-toned modelling paste
100 g light pink modelling paste
70 g flame-red modelling paste
50 g light butter-yellow modelling paste
40 g buttercup-yellow modelling paste
25 g moss-green modelling paste
unbreakable lace in pink and yellow (p. 36)
brown dusting powder
cream edible glitter
pink edible glitter
white gel colour
ivory gel colour
shortening
clear alcohol or lemon juice
non-toxic glue
edible glue
22 white dragées
support sticks

Preparation

UP TO A WEEK IN ADVANCE:

Cover the cake board with 550 g moss-green fondant. Roll a bubble impression roller around the edges of the board to add texture. Glue a ribbon around the edge of the board using non-toxic glue and set aside to dry.

Make two fairies. One lying on her tummy and the other sitting up.

Make 13 toadstools in various sizes, 11 white primula blossoms, 11 tiny yellow blossoms (see page 33) and four butterflies.

Make two sets of fairy wings.

ONE DAY IN ADVANCE:

Bake the cake layers, and allow to cool and settle for at least 6 hours. Level each layer; fill and stack the cakes. Cover the cake in white chocolate ganache and allow to set overnight.

TREE STUMP

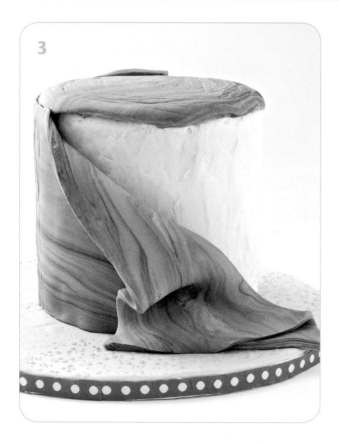

1. Marble the light and dark brown fondants and roll out to a thickness of 3 mm. Cut a 15 cm circle out of the rolled fondant using the cake tin the cakes were baked in.
2. Brush the surface of the ganached cake with clear alcohol or lemon juice.

3. Drape the circle of fondant over the top and sides of the cake. Smooth the fondant surface with a fondant smoother or a ball of leftover fondant.
4. Create the wood grain in the fondant with a veining tool.

TOADSTOOLS

1. Roll 5 g flame-red and 5 g white modelling paste into a smooth ball. Shape the flame-red ball into a cone. Roll 2 g white modelling paste into a ball, then press into a small circle.

2. Roll the white ball into a short sausage, one end narrower than the other. Roll another thin sausage of white modelling paste and wrap it around the sausage as shown. Secure with a little edible glue.

3. Stick the white circle onto the base of the red cone with edible glue. Make grooves in a radiating pattern with a toothpick in the white paste for the underside of the toadstool cap.

4. Stick the end of a paintbrush into the centre of the base of the toadstool cap and glue the narrower end of the toadstool body into this hole. Paint dots on the top of the toadstool with a toothpick dipped in white gel colour.

ROOTS

1. Roll leftover brown fondant into long sausages and stick onto the side of the cake with edible glue, positioning them to look like tree roots.

2. Mark the wood grain on the roots with a sharp knife, matching it with the wood grain on the rest of the cake.

3. Brush brown dusting powder over the surface of the cake with a large dusting brush to emphasise the wood grain.

BUTTERFLIES

1. Roll 20 g white modelling paste to a thickness of 0.5 mm. The paste should be transparent.

2. Allow the paste to sit uncovered for 8–10 minutes.

3. Cut out four butterflies with a butterfly paper punch (the type used for scrapbooking).

4. Brush each butterfly with a little edible glue and sprinkle over a little pink edible glitter.

PINK FLOWER FAIRY

1. Make two legs with 10 g flesh-toned modelling paste using the technique on page 36.

2. Position the legs in a sitting position over the edge of a Styrofoam cake dummy. Glue the tops of the legs together with a little edible glue. Insert a support stick where the legs meet down into the cake dummy. This will later anchor the fairy onto the cake.

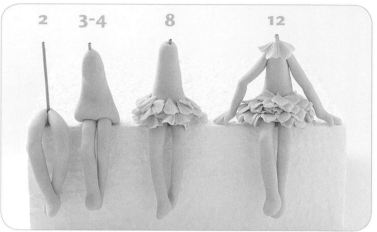

3. Shape 18 g light pink modelling paste into an elongated teardrop. Push the wider end onto the support stick to position the body over the top of the legs, and secure with some edible glue. Make sure the support stick protrudes out of the top of the body. If not, insert a second support stick.

4. Mark folds on the body with the back of a knife blade.

5. Roll out 50 g light pink modelling paste to a thickness of about 2 mm. Cut out 13 medium blossoms using a five-petal blossom cutter.

6. Press each blossom, one at a time, into a five-petal blossom veiner.

7. Cut out one petal from each of the blossoms with a sharp knife. Keep these single petals to fill in any gaps on the skirt. Leave one blossom whole to be used as a collar for the dress. Open each blossom by widening the gap where the petal was removed.

8. Glue these blossoms to the base of the body in three or four layers. First glue a blossom to each side of the body with the tips of the petals facing outwards. Then stick a blossom to the rear of the body and finally the front. Repeat this for another two layers. Fill in any gaps in the skirt with the single petals. The skirt should finish at the waist of the body.

9. Make two arms with 8 g flesh-toned modelling paste using the technique on page 35.

10. Push the hands on each arm out at the wrist. Pinch the wrist of each hand between two fingers to give the hand definition.

11. Attach each arm to the top of the fairy body. Position the hands on either side of the skirt, touching the cake dummy.

12. Brush the shoulders with a little edible glue and thread the set-aside whole blossom over the support stick. Position the blossom to cover the places where the arms are joined to the body.

13. Roll 15 g flesh-toned modelling paste into a smooth ball. Shape the fairy face using the technique on page 34. While painting the eyebrows with ivory gel colour, paint three freckles on each cheek with the tip of a toothpick.

14. Glue the head onto the support stick with edible glue. Allow the head to dry for a few hours before adding the hair.

15. Make a set of pink fairy wings using the technique on page 36 and the template on page 143.

16. For the hair, mix shortening with 25 g flesh-toned modelling paste. Marble the flesh tone with

10 g light butter-yellow modelling paste. When the paste is extruded, the hair will have a natural look with a mixture of tints and highlights.

17. Follow the technique on page 34 and create long hair with a short fringe for the fairy. Finish her hair with a tiny blossom.
18. Attach the cut-out wings onto the fairy with a dot of royal icing.

YELLOW FLOWER FAIRY

1. Model the fairy in the same way as the pink fairy and position her legs, body and arms so that she is lying on her tummy.
2. Create a skirt using the technique used for the baby in a teacup cake on page 43, but use buttercup-yellow modelling paste.

3. Make a set of yellow fairy wings using the technique on page 36 and the template on page 143 and attach to the fairy with a dot of royal icing.

TENDRILS

1. Mix a small amount of shortening with 25 g moss-green modelling paste.
2. Place the paste into an extruder. Extrude 12 cm lengths of paste through a small-holed disk extruder.
3. Wrap each length of paste around a toothpick and allow to set for about 5–10 minutes.
4. Carefully remove the tendrils of paste from the toothpicks; they will hold their shape.

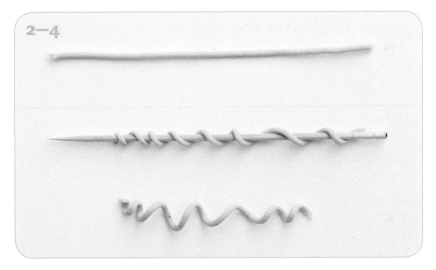

ASSEMBLY

1. Stick the toadstools in clusters around the edge of the stump, using the wet royal icing to secure them to the cake board.
2. Fill an icing bag with dark and light moss-green royal icing. Attach a grass tube and pipe grass around the base of the tree stump and around the tree roots and toadstools.
3. Attach the tendrils and flowers onto the tree stump and the cake board. Top a few flowers and

toadstools with butterflies, using edible glue to attach them.
4. Glue the fairies into position on the tree stump and the front of the cake board.
5. Dip a large, dry paintbrush into edible cream glitter and dust each fairy with a little glitter to give her an enchanted appearance.

Hamburger cake

My father used to make hamburgers from scratch every Friday night when I was
growing up. This is the cake I would have made for his 70th birthday
if he had lived a little closer.

Recipes

- 1 quantity vanilla bean sponge baked in three 20 cm round cake tins (p. 19)
- 1 quantity dark chocolate ganache (p. 23)

EQUIPMENT

large and small rolling pins
4 cm square cutter
sharp knife
flat brush
palette knife
bowl
1 cm circle cutter
3.7 cm circle cutter
4 cm circle cutter
6 cm circle cutter
5 cm five-petal cutter
leaf-vein impression mat
toothpicks

MATERIALS

35 cm square cake board
ribbon
700 g butter-yellow fondant
150 g white fondant
180 g flame-red fondant
150 g pink fondant
60 g buttercup-yellow fondant
60 g lime-green fondant
60 g mustard-yellow fondant
30 g coral fondant
30 g white modelling paste
lime-green gel colour
brown, apricot and buttercup-yellow petal dust
rubine dusting powder
non-toxic glue
edible glue
clear alcohol or lemon juice
non-stick bake spray

Preparation

ONE DAY OR UP TO A WEEK IN ADVANCE:

Cover the cake board to look like a gingham tablecloth. Glue the ribbon around the edge of the board and set aside to dry.

ONE DAY IN ADVANCE:

Bake the cake layers, and allow them to cool and settle.

CAKE BOARD

1. Roll out 150 g white fondant to a thickness of 2 mm. Repeat with 150 g flame-red and 150 g pink fondant.
2. Cut out 16 squares of red, 16 squares of pink and 25 squares of white fondant using a 4 cm square cutter.
3. Brush the board with water or edible glue.
4. Begin at the top right corner of the board and paste down one red square. Lay out the board in a gingham pattern as shown (see photo above).
5. Dust rubine dusting powder on the outer edges of the pink squares with a flat brush.
6. Stick the ribbon along the edge of the board with non-toxic glue. Allow the board to dry.

CAKE

1. Carve two cake layers to resemble the top and bottom of a hamburger bun. Shape the third cake to resemble a hamburger patty.
2. Ganache the two hamburger bun cakes and set aside for the ganache to set.
3. Cover the hamburger patty cake with ganache. Allow the ganache to set for 15 minutes before covering with a second layer. Rough up the ganache with a palette knife to make the cake look like a cooked hamburger patty.
4. Place the cake for the bottom of the hamburger bun on an upturned bowl. This will allow you to tuck the fondant under the cake. Brush the bun cake with clear alcohol or lemon juice.
5. Roll out 350 g butter-yellow fondant to 2 mm thick. Cover the bun in fondant, taking care to tuck the fondant under the cake. Trim excess fondant. Repeat with the top bun.

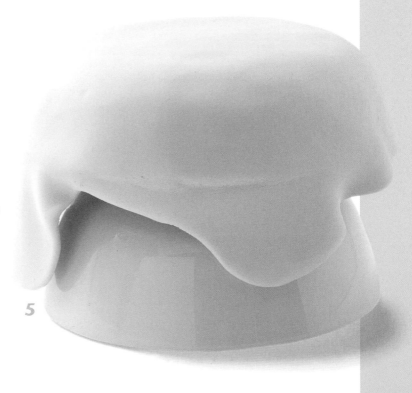

CHEESE SLICES

1. Roll out 60 g buttercup-yellow fondant to a thickness of 3 mm.
2. Cut out a 10 x 10 cm square. Cut the square in half diagonally to create two triangles.
3. Cut out small holes in the fondant with a 1 cm circle cutter. Cut away half circles from the sides in a random pattern.
4. Place the cheese slices directly onto the hamburger cake, so the fondant will drape over the edge for a natural look.

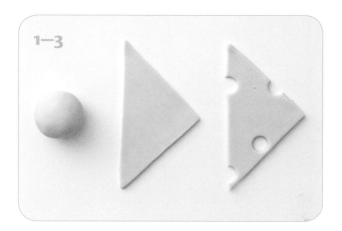

TOMATO SLICES

1. Roll out 30 g flame-red fondant to a thickness of 3 mm. Cut out a 6 cm circle.
2. Cut out the centre of the circle with a 5 cm five-petal cutter.
3. Roll out 30 g coral fondant to a thickness of 3 mm. Cut out a 5 cm five-petal flower.
4. Slot the coral flower into the space in the flame-red circle.
5. Roll tiny balls of coral fondant for tomato seeds. Cut the slice in half.

LETTUCE

1. Roll out 60 g lime-green fondant to a thickness of 1 mm.
2. Press a leaf-vein impression mat into the fondant.
3. Frill the edge of the fondant with a toothpick and create folds in the lettuce as shown.

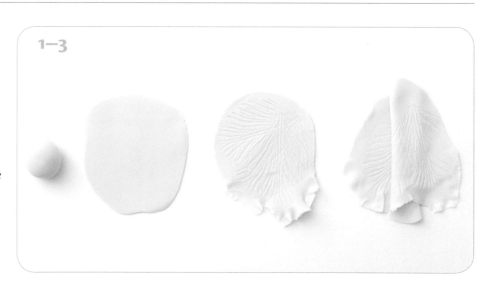

ONION

1. Roll out 30 g white modelling paste to a thickness of 3 mm. Cut out a 4 cm circle.
2. Press a 3.7 cm circle cutter in the centre and cut out the centre to create a ring.
3. Dip the tip of a toothpick into lime-green gel colour and paint lines randomly on the ring to make it look more onion-like.

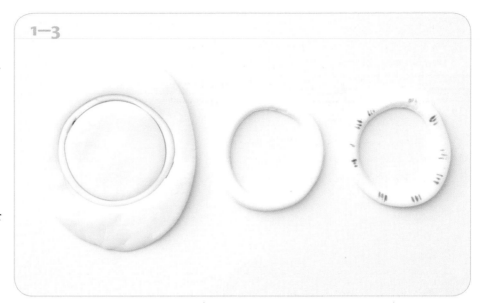

ASSEMBLY

1. Place the bottom bun cake just off-centre on the prepared cake board. Assemble the fondant lettuce around the edge.
2. Place the hamburger patty cake with the cheese slice on top of the bun cake.
3. Top with prepared tomato slices and onion rings and finish off with the top bun cake.
4. Dust the bun cakes with a mixture of brown, apricot and buttercup-yellow petal dust.
5. Make tiny sesame seeds from leftover butter-yellow fondant and attach with edible glue.
6. Spray the top bun cake with bake spray for a glazed look.
7. Roll 60 g mustard-yellow fondant into long thin ropes and use to write the name on the cake board.

Braai cake

My husband is the world's best 'braaier' (barbecuer). This is his dream cake and it serves up very easily. Each guest removes a brick of cake to enjoy at the end of an informal braai party.

Recipes

- 3 quantities vanilla bean sponge baked in a 30 x 30 cm cake tin (p. 19)
- 2 quantities white chocolate ganache (p. 23)
- 1 quantity royal icing (p. 25)

EQUIPMENT

large and small rolling pins
long palette knife
1.5 cm square cutter
large and small soft paintbrushes
toothpicks
sharp knife

MATERIALS

30 cm square cake board
ribbon
550 g terracotta fondant
800 g brown fondant
80 g chocolate-brown fondant
240 g light flesh-toned modelling paste
180 g red modelling paste
180 g moss-green modelling paste
200 g off-white modelling paste
40 g light grey modelling paste
40 g dark grey modelling paste
40 g black modelling paste
40 g orange modelling paste
20 g light brown modelling paste
brown dusting powder
ivory gel colour
edible orange glitter
non-toxic glue
edible glue
clear alcohol or lemon juice
15 x 15 cm black plastic fencing
4 kebab sticks

Preparation

ONE WEEK IN ADVANCE:
Cover the board and make the kebabs.

ONE DAY IN ADVANCE:
Bake the cake and make the ganache.

CAKE BOARD

1. Roll out 550 g terracotta fondant to 2 mm thick and cover the cake board.
2. Score a crosshatch pattern into the fondant with the back of a long palette knife as shown. Where each line crosses, cut out squares using a 1.5 cm square cutter.
3. Roll out 80 g chocolate-brown fondant to a thickness of 2 mm. Cut out 1.5 cm squares using the same cutter. Replace the removed terracotta squares with the chocolate-brown ones.
4. Dust brown dusting powder around the edges of each tile.
5. Glue ribbon around the edge of the board with non-toxic glue and set aside to dry.

KEBABS

1. Divide and shape 80 g light flesh-toned modelling paste into two chicken cubes.
2. Divide and shape 60 g red modelling paste into two red pepper pieces. Do the same with 60 g moss-green modelling paste.
3. To make mushrooms, shape 60 g off-white modelling paste into a dome. Press 20 g light brown modelling paste into a circle and glue to the underside of the dome with edible glue. Mark grooves in the circle with a toothpick. Roll a short sausage shape from 5 g off-white modelling paste. Glue this to the centre of the brown circle with edible glue to finish off the mushroom.
4. Thread a kebab stick with a green pepper, a red pepper, a cube of chicken and a mushroom, followed by a second piece of red pepper, a cube of chicken and a green pepper.
5. Brush ivory gel colour along the length of a second kebab stick. Press the painted stick over the kebabs to create a grill pattern. Make two more kebabs in the same way.

1–4

GLOWING COALS

1. Roll 40 g each of light grey, dark grey, black and orange modelling paste into long sausage shapes.
2. Lay the sausages side by side.
3. Twist the four colours together and mix to form a marbled lump of paste.
4. Cut rough shapes from the lump with a sharp knife.

5. Brush the coals with edible glue and dust with a small amount of edible orange glitter.

BRAAI BRICKS

1. Cut the cake into rectangles measuring 10 x 5 cm.
2. Cover each rectangle in ganache.
3. Roll out 100 g brown fondant to a thickness of 2 mm and cut out a 13 x 8 cm rectangle.
4. Brush the ganache of a cake rectangle with clear alcohol or lemon juice. Place the ganached cake in the centre of the fondant.
5. Fold the fondant around the cake, tucking in the edges. Turn over the cake and trim any excess fondant where necessary.

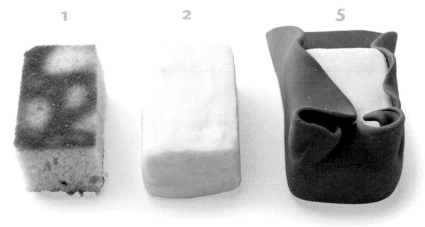

6. Rough the sides of the fondant to give a realistic 'brick' look and dust with brown dusting powder. Repeat with the rest of the ganached cakes.

ASSEMBLY

1. Arrange five cake bricks in a circle in the centre of the prepared cake board. Arrange the remaining cake bricks on top, with the second layer resting on the ends of the bricks of the previous layer as shown.
2. Position the glowing coals in the centre of the bricks, placing a few outside the circle.
3. Place the plastic fencing for the braai grid on top of the bricks, securing it with small dots of royal icing.
4. Position the kebabs on the grid to finish.

Handbag cake

I can never have too many handbags and shoes. This handbag cake is perfect for the woman who has everything; it would make a fantastic gift, boxed in a large gift box and hand delivered.

Recipes

- 1 quantity vanilla bean sponge (p. 19) OR ½ quantity double chocolate cake (p. 18) baked in two 20 cm round cake tins
- 1 quantity white chocolate ganache (p. 23)
- 1 quantity vanilla buttercream (p. 21)
- ½ quantity royal icing (p. 25)

EQUIPMENT

large and small rolling pins
paisley impression mat
plastic clingfilm
medium calyx cutter
medium rose leaf plunger cutter
small soft paintbrush
fondant smoother
toothpicks
sharp knife
extruder
roll of kitchen towel
Styrofoam cake dummy
templates for handbag, flap and handle (p. 148, 143 and 147)
baking paper
pair of scissors
serrated knife
veining tool
quilting wheel
extruder
sponge

MATERIALS

30 cm round cake board
ribbon
550 g white fondant
1 kg light lime-green fondant
240 g light lime-green modelling paste
100 g lemon-yellow flower paste
100 g lime-green flower paste
lemon-yellow petal dust
lemon-yellow lustre dust
shortening
non-toxic glue
edible glue
clear alcohol or lemon juice

Preparation

UP TO A WEEK IN ADVANCE:
Make 12 free-form roses and 26 medium rose leaves using the techniques on page 46.
Make the handbag handle and clasp.
Cover the cake board in 550 g white fondant. Emboss with the paisley impression mat. Glue the ribbon
around the edge of the board with non-toxic glue. Set aside and allow to dry.

ONE DAY IN ADVANCE:
Bake the cake layers, and allow to cool and settle for at least 6 hours.
Level, fill and stack the layers.

ROSES

1. Make 12 small free-form roses from 100 g lemon-yellow flower paste using the technique on page 46.

2. Make the calyx using 50 g lime-green flower paste as shown on page 46.
3. Dust each rose with lemon-yellow petal dust.

ROSE LEAVES

1. Roll out 50 g lime-green flower paste to a thickness of 1 mm.

2. Cut 26 rose leaves with a medium rose leaf plunger cutter. Shape each leaf before drying as shown on page 46.

HANDBAG HANDLE

1. Roll 150 g light lime-green modelling paste into a smooth ball.
2. Roll the ball into a long, smooth sausage with the flat side of a fondant smoother; this will give an even width.
3. Flatten the ends of the sausage with the fondant smoother and flatten one edge of the handle in the same way.

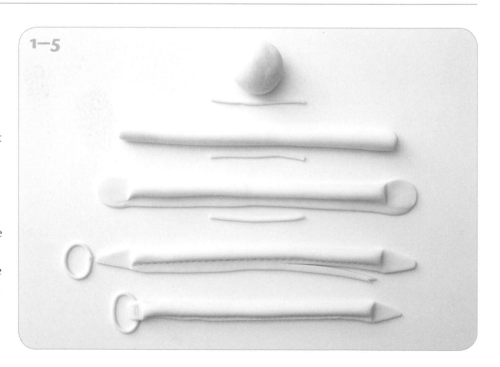

1–5

4. Mark a row of stitches with the tip of a toothpick. Trim away excess fondant along the flattened side of the handle and cut each end to a point.

5. Mix 25 g light lime-green modelling paste with a little shortening. Extrude two 10 cm ropes of paste from an extruder. Loop each rope and glue the ends together with edible glue. Place the loops under each end of the handle. Tuck the ends of the handle around the loops. Add stitch detail with the tip of a toothpick.

6. Drape the handle over a roll of kitchen towel and rest the roll on a Styrofoam cake dummy. This forms the arch for the handbag handle and allows the ends of the handle to hang down without touching anything. Allow the handle to dry for at least 24 hours. The handle is more fragile when it is still wet.

CLASP

1. Roll 10 g light lime-green modelling paste into a smooth ball.
2. Roll the ball into a 4 cm-long sausage.
3. Mark ridges with the back of a knife.

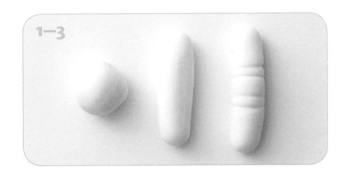

SCULPTING THE CAKE

1. Trace the handbag template on page 148 onto baking paper. Cut out the template and place it on top of the cake. Cut around the template with a serrated knife. Set the template aside to use when covering the cake.

2. Turn the cake onto the flat edge and cover in white chocolate ganache. Allow the ganache to set overnight.

COVERING THE CAKE

1. Roll out 450 g light lime-green fondant in a rectangular shape at least 45 cm long and to a thickness of 2 mm.
2. Measure the width of the cake and cut a strip of fondant this width.
3. Brush the surface of the cake with clear alcohol or lemon juice.
4. Cover the top and sides of the cake with the strip of fondant, trimming and tucking the edges under the cake.

5. Roll out 300 g light lime-green fondant to a thickness of 2 mm. Using the template from sculpturing the cake, cut out a piece of fondant with a sharp knife to cover the front of the cake. Place the cut-out fondant on the front, smoothing it with a fondant smoother or a ball of excess fondant. Repeat with the remaining light lime-green fondant to cover the rear of the cake.
6. Mark folds in the bag with a veining tool.
7. Roll out the remaining light lime-green fondant and cut out the bag flap using the template on page 143.
8. Drape the flap over the top of the bag. Mark stitching on the back edge of the flap with the tip of a toothpick or a quilting wheel.
9. Mix some shortening with 50 g light lime-green modelling paste. Place the paste in an extruder and extrude a half-circle rope of paste. Use the extruded paste to cover the joins along the sides of the cake as shown. Stick down with edible glue.
10. Attach the roses to the front of the bag with a little royal icing. Tuck the rose leaves under the roses and attach in the same way.

ATTACHING THE HANDLE

1. Roll out any remaining light lime-green fondant to a thickness of 2 mm. Cut out two rectangular shapes measuring 3 x 1.5 cm. Mark with stitching around the edges. These will be used to attach the handle to the bag.

2. Place the dried handle in position on the top of the handbag and use a small amount of royal icing to hold it in place. Prop up the handle with a sponge to allow the royal icing to dry.

3. Place one prepared rectangle of fondant over the loop of the handle and glue in place with a little edible glue. Repeat on the other side of the handle.

4. Dust the top of the bag and handle with a little lemon-yellow lustre dust to finish off the cake.

TIP

For a fun and funky handbag, replace the roses with the daisies from the quilted daisy cake (see page 48). Use cerise and orange paste to create the daisies. This will make the handbag suitable for someone younger.

Castle cake

I first made this cake for my daughter's fourth birthday party. She had begged for a castle cake and I wanted to create a unique shape that would still be recognisable as a castle.

Recipes

- 1 quantity double chocolate cake baked in two 20 cm square cake tins (p. 18)
- 1 quantity dark chocolate ganache (p. 23)
- 1 quantity chocolate buttercream (variations p. 21)
- ½ quantity royal icing (p. 25)

EQUIPMENT

small and large rolling pins
small and large paintbrushes
sharp knife
toothpicks
small daisy plunger cutter
fondant smoother
2.5 cm circle cutter
6 cm circle cutter
2 cm square cutter

MATERIALS

30 cm square cake board
ribbon
15 cm PVC piping (5.5 cm diameter), cut in half
1.2 kg apricot fondant
500 g moss-green fondant
400 g light pink fondant
200 g light blue modelling paste
200 g light pink modelling paste
200 g dark pink modelling paste
200 g apricot modelling paste
200 g white modelling paste
10 g brown modelling paste
10 g light lime-green modelling paste
6 g dark lime-green modelling paste
10 pink pearl dragées
5 ml fondant sand (p. 32)
pearl lustre dust
ivory gel colour
non-toxic glue
edible glue
clear alcohol or lemon juice

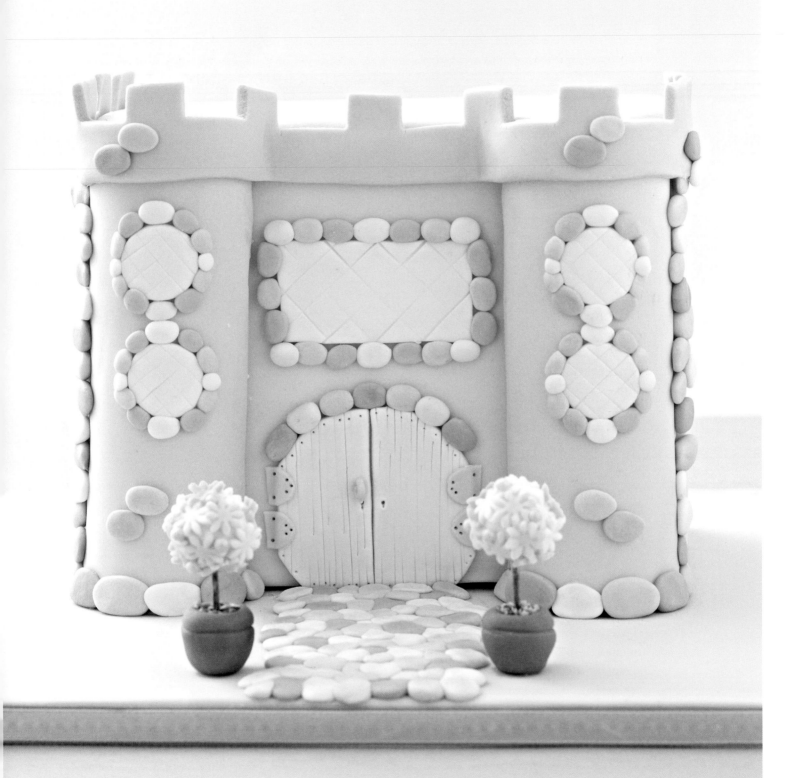

Preparation

UP TO A WEEK IN ADVANCE:

Cover the cake board in 500 g moss-green fondant. Glue a ribbon around the edge
of the board with non-toxic glue.
Make the topiary trees.

ONE DAY IN ADVANCE:

Bake the cake layers, and allow to cool and settle for at least 6 hours. Cut each layer in half creating four
10 x 20 cm cakes and stack the halves to a height of 15 cm. Cover the cake with ganache and allow to set.

TOPIARY TREES

1. For each topiary tree, roll a 5 g ball of brown modelling paste, a 4 g ball of light lime-green modelling paste, a 3 g ball of light lime-green modelling paste and a 3 g ball of dark lime-green modelling paste.
2. To create the pot, flatten the bottom of the ball of brown paste and make a hollow with the back of a paintbrush. Run the back of a knife along the open edge to create a lip.
3. Thinly roll out the smaller balls of light and dark lime-green paste and cut out 10 daisies from each with a small daisy plunger cutter.
4. Push the larger ball of light lime-green paste onto the end of a toothpick and secure with a little edible glue. Stick the daisy shapes onto it, taking care to cover the entire ball.
5. Stick five pink pearl dragées among the daisies.

6. Paint the toothpick brown with a damp paintbrush dipped in ivory gel colour. Stick the bottom of the toothpick into the pot, securing it with edible glue.

7. Spoon about a quarter of a teaspoon of fondant sand into the plant pot to complete the topiary tree. Make a second tree in the same way.

CASTLE TURRETS

1. Brush the sides of each PVC pipe with edible glue.
2. Roll out 400 g apricot fondant to a thickness of 2 mm. Cut the rolled-out fondant in half.
3. Drape one piece over a pipe and smooth with a spare piece of fondant. Cover the second pipe in the same way.

DECORATING THE CASTLE

1. Paint the surface of the ganached cake with clear alcohol or lemon juice.
2. Roll out 450 g apricot fondant to a thickness of 2 mm. Measure the side of the cake and cut four matching panels of apricot fondant. Place the panels onto the sides of the cake, smoothing the surface with a fondant smoother.
3. Roll out 300 g apricot fondant to a thickness of 2 mm. Measure the top of the cake and cut out a matching panel of fondant. Place the fondant onto the top of the cake and smooth with a fondant smoother.
4. Place the cake on the cake board and attach the turrets to the front of the cake, securing them with royal icing.
5. Cut a 6 cm circle from the remaining apricot fondant and halve it with a sharp knife. Cover the top of each turret with a half circle of fondant.

1—3

COBBLESTONES

1. Roll pea-sized balls of light blue, apricot, light pink and dark pink modelling paste.
2. Push these balls onto the board to create a pathway leading up to the castle door.

WINDOWS

1. Roll out 200 g of white modelling paste to a thickness of 2 mm. Cut four 2.5 cm circles and a 7 x 3 cm rectangle from rolled-out white modelling paste.
2. Score a crosshatch pattern on the surface of each shape.
3. Dust with pearl lustre dust before sticking them onto the cake.
4. Roll pea-sized balls of modelling paste as for the cobblestones and stick them around each window to create stone borders.

DOOR

1. Roll out the remaining light blue modelling paste to a thickness of 2 mm. Cut out a 6 cm circle. Cut a small section off the circle to form the base of the door, and then cut straight sides.
2. Mark the centre of the door with the back of a knife and create a wood-grain effect with a sharp knife.
3. Stick the door in place with edible glue.
4. Cut hinges from rolled-out apricot modelling paste and stick them onto the door with edible glue. Create a door handle from a tiny sausage of apricot modelling paste and attach to the door with edible glue. Mark nails in the hinges and door with the tip of a toothpick.
5. Position the topiary trees on either side of the door.

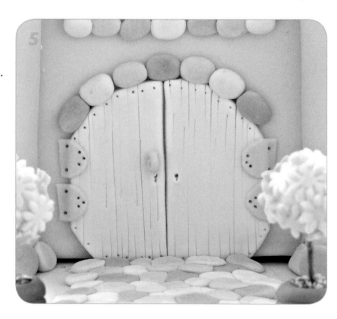

TOP TRIM

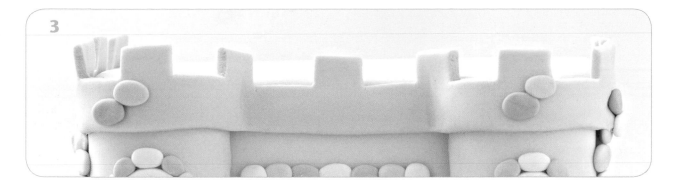

1. Roll out 400 g light pink fondant to a thickness of 5 mm. Cut three strips 3 cm wide.
2. Cut out 2 cm squares from one edge as shown, spacing the cut-outs evenly.
3. Glue the strips around the top of the cake with edible glue or royal icing allowing half to protrude above the top. Smooth the joins so that the trim appears seamless.

STONE DETAILS

1. Roll balls of light blue, apricot, light pink and dark pink modelling paste into oblong stone shapes.
2. Use these to decorate the sides of the turrets, above the door and around the base of the cake.

TIP
If time allows, dust the PVC pipes with cornflour before making the turrets as shown. Allow them to dry for about 10 hours or until completely dry and remove the fondant from the PVC pipe before using them for the cake. For an added surprise fill the turrets with small sweets.

Farmyard cake

Using the whimsical shape of a topsy-turvy cake gives this popular themed cake a little added character. If time allows, create enough farm animals for each child at the party to be able to have his or her own one to take home.

Recipes

- 1½ quantities double chocolate cake baked in three 20 cm square cake tins (p. 18)
- ¾ quantity double chocolate cake baked in three 15 cm square cake tins (p. 18)
- 3 quantities dark chocolate ganache (p. 23)
- ½ quantity royal icing (p. 25)

EQUIPMENT

large and small rolling pins
bubble texture roller
sharp knife
toothpicks
veining tool
bone tool
nail scissors
fondant smoother
daisy plunger cutter
various blossom cutters
five-petal blossom cutter
blossom veiner
icing bag
grass tube

MATERIALS

35 cm round cake board
ribbon
1.2 kg lime-green fondant
600 g white fondant
900 g light brown fondant
300 g white modelling paste
140 g light pink modelling paste
60 g yellow modelling paste
50 g brown modelling paste
30 g flame-red modelling paste
30 g orange modelling paste
20 g black modelling paste
lime-green dusting powder
light pink dusting powder
buttercup-yellow dusting powder
white gel colour
non-toxic glue
edible glue
support sticks
yellow and white dragées
clear alcohol or lemon juice

Preparation

UP TO A WEEK IN ADVANCE:
Cover the cake board.
Model the animals and a selection of small daisies, blossoms and primulas (see page 33).

TWO DAYS IN ADVANCE:
Bake the cake layers.

ONE DAY IN ADVANCE:
Level the cake layers, and stack and fill the three 20 cm cakes to make the bottom tier and the three 15 cm cakes to make the top tier.
Carve each cake into a topsy-turvy shape using the technique on page 27. Cover both cakes in ganache and set aside to allow the ganache to become firm overnight.

CAKE BOARD

1. Cover the cake board in 550 g lime-green fondant.
2. Emboss the edges of the board with a bubble texture roller and dust with lime-green dusting powder.
3. Stick a ribbon around the edge of the board with non-toxic glue and set aside to dry.

COW

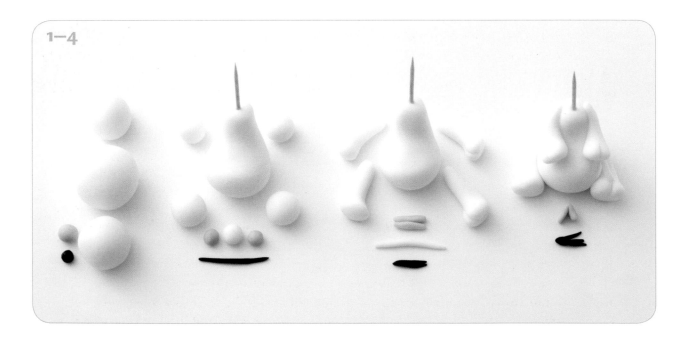

1–4

1. For the body, roll three balls of white modelling paste, 40 g, 10 g and 8g.
2. Shape the largest ball into a calabash and insert a support stick at the narrow end. Divide each smaller ball into two and shape into arms and legs as shown.
3. Mark the hooves with the back of a knife.
4. Attach the arms and legs on either side of the body with edible glue.
5. For the tail, roll 6 g white modelling paste into one thin sausage and 4 g black modelling paste into two thin sausages. Taper the ends of the black sausages, fold in half and attach the four strands to the end of the white sausage with edible glue. Attach the tail to the cow's rear and bring it around the body to rest on one leg.
6. Halve 3 g light pink modelling paste and roll two tiny sausages. Place side by side and fold each in half to form the udders. Glue onto the cow with edible glue.
7. For the head, roll three balls of white modelling paste, 30 g, 3 g and 3 g.
8. Shape the larger ball into a calabash and the two smaller balls into teardrops for the ears. Flatten the ears and press a bone tool into the wide end of each. Roll the shapes as shown. Attach the ears to the side of the head with edible glue.
9. Mark the eyes with the tip of a toothpick and the nostrils with the large end of a veining tool.

Use the tool in reverse to create domed nostrils and emphasise them by pulling the edge of the tool around each hole. Mark the mouth with the veining tool.

10. Roll two tiny balls of black modelling paste for the eyes and stick these over the eye markings. Mark the glint in each eye on the top right-hand corner with white gel colour on the end of a toothpick.
11. Brush the body's support stick with edible glue and position the head on top.
12. Dust the nostrils with light pink dusting powder.
13. Make the second cow in the same way, but position it so that it is lying on its side.

PIG

1. For the body, roll three balls of light pink modelling paste, 20 g, 10 g and 8g (see overleaf for photo of steps 1–4).
2. Shape the largest ball into a calabash and insert a support stick at the narrow end. Divide each smaller ball into two and shape into arms and legs as shown.
3. Mark the belly button with a toothpick. Mark the hooves and folds on the body with the back of a knife.
4. Attach the arms and legs on either side of the body with edible glue. Make a little curly tail using a short thin sausage of light pink modelling paste and attach to the pig's rear.

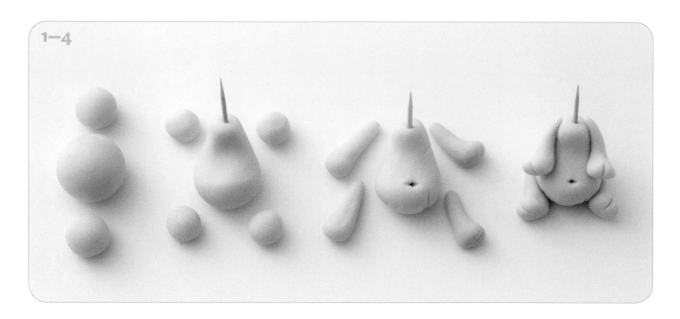

5. For the head, roll four balls of light pink modelling paste, 20 g, 3 g, 2 g and 2 g.

6. Shape the larger ball into a cone and the two smallest balls into teardrops for the ears. Press a veining tool into each ear and pinch the tips to points. Flatten the 3 g ball to create a snout.

7. Glue the snout onto the centre of the face with edible glue and mark two nostrils with a veining tool. Similarly mark the mouth under the snout. Mark the eyes with a toothpick. Attach the ears to the side of the head with edible glue.

8. For the mouth, insert the larger point of the veining tool under the snout and pull down and forward in one motion.

9. Roll two tiny balls of black modelling paste for the eyes and stick these over the eye markings. Mark the glint in each eye on the top right-hand corner with white gel colour on the end of a toothpick.

10. Brush the body's support stick with edible glue and position the head on top.

11. Dust the nostrils with light pink dusting powder.

12. Make a second pig in the same way, but position him so that he is lying on his back. As a fun extra, make two pig bottoms with curly tails and glue them onto a 'puddle' of mud to make it look like they're wallowing.

CHICKENS

1. Roll four balls of white modelling paste, 10 g, 5 g, 5 g and 5 g.

2. Shape the largest ball into the body of the chicken and insert a support stick at the neck end. Roll two of the smaller balls into teardrops and flatten slightly. Cut into the teardrops with a sharp knife and shape as shown to form the wings.

3. Thinly roll out a little additional white and a little flame-red modelling paste. Cut a small daisy from each using a daisy plunger cutter. Cut three petals from the red daisy.

4. Thread the white daisy over the support stick and onto the shoulders of the body. Dust the daisy with buttercup-yellow dusting powder.

5. Brush the body's support stick with edible glue and position the head on top. Mark eyes with a toothpick. Roll a tiny amount of orange modelling paste into a triangular shape. Cut into the paste with a pair of nail scissors to make a beak.

6. Attach the beak to the front of the head with edible glue. Roll two tiny balls of black modelling paste for the eyes and stick these over the eye markings.

7. Glue the three red petals to the top of the head and attach the wings to the sides of the body with edible glue.

8. Repeat to make a second chicken. Make the rooster by adding two flame-red daisy petals under the beak and a yellow, red and orange tail.

COVERING THE CAKES

1. Brush the surface of the ganached cakes with clear alcohol or lemon juice.
2. Roll out 600 g white fondant to a thickness of 2 mm. Lay one side of the smaller cake on top of the fondant and trim around it with a sharp knife. Lift the cake and smooth the fondant with a fondant smoother.
3. Repeat with the second side, the rear and finally the front of the cake, until the four sides are covered in white fondant.
4. Mark wood panels and wood grain with a sharp knife. Use the tip of a toothpick to make nail marks.
5. Roll out the remaining lime-green fondant and cover the larger cake in the same way, but leave the surface of this one smooth. Place on the cake board and position the coop on top, securing it with royal icing.

CHICKEN COOP ROOF

1. Roll out 500 g light brown fondant to a thickness of 2 mm.
2. Cut out five-petal blossoms with a five-petal blossom cutter and arrange on the roof of the chicken coop in overlapping rows to create tiles. Secure them with edible glue.

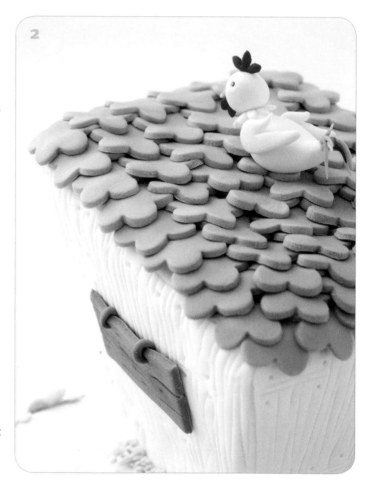

FLAP

1. Roll out any leftover brown fondant to a thickness of 2 mm. Cut out a rectangle measuring roughly 6 cm x 3 cm.
2. With the back of a knife, mark the fondant with long parallel marks to create a wood-grain effect.
3. Attach to the chicken coop with a little edible glue.
4. Roll two tiny balls of brown fondant into short sausage shapes and bend each to form a small loop.
5. Attach each loop to the top of the fondant flap to create hinges. Dust some brown petal dust over the flap to enhance the wood-grain effect.

PICKET FENCE

1. Roll out 400 g light brown fondant to a thickness of 3 mm. Cut 28 strips of fondant measuring 5 cm x 1.5 cm.
2. Mark each strip with wood grain with the back of a knife and use the tip of a toothpick or paintbrush handle to mark nails into each strip.
3. Arrange the strips on the base of the bottom tier to make a fence that runs around the cake. Secure with a little edible glue.

ASSEMBLY

1. Fill an icing bag with dark and light moss-green royal icing. With a grass tube, pipe grass around the base of the bottom tier and the coop.
2. Attach the daisies and blossoms with edible glue using the picture as a guide.
3. Position the animals on the cake board and the chickens and rooster on the cake, securing each with edible glue.

African explorer cake

This backpack cake is a twist on the traditional wild animal cake
that is so popular with young children.

Recipes

- 1½ quantities double chocolate cake baked in four 20 cm round cake tins (p. 18)
- 1 quantity dark chocolate ganache (p. 23)
- 1 quantity chocolate buttercream (variations p. 21)
- ⅓ quantity royal icing (p. 25)

EQUIPMENT

large and small rolling pins
toothpicks
veining tool
bone tool
kebab stick
large and small paintbrushes
medium multi-hole disk extruder
support stick
sharp knife
3 straws of different diameters
quilting wheel tool
templates for pocket, knapsack flap, handle and straps
(p. 146 and 147)
baking paper
2 cm round cutter

MATERIALS

35 cm round cake board
ribbon
1.5 kg brown fondant
400 g blue fondant
100 g yellow modelling paste
100 g brown modelling paste
80 g grey modelling paste
70 g white modelling paste
55 g orange modelling paste
30 g black modelling paste
5 g light pink modelling paste
10 black stamens
brown gel colour
ivory gel colour
black edible ink marker
brown dusting powder
fondant sand (p. 32)
non-toxic glue
edible glue
shortening
clear alcohol or lemon juice
unbreakable lace in light blue (p. 36)

Preparation

TWO DAYS OR UP TO A WEEK IN ADVANCE:

Cover the cake board in 400 g blue fondant. Glue the ribbon around the edge with non-toxic glue.
Make the animal faces and the monkey (leave the right arm to finish when the monkey is placed on the cake).
Make the dragonfly wings with unbreakable lace (see recipe on page 36). Allow to dry and
cut out four wings using the template on page 147.
Keep in a dry place until needed.

ONE DAY IN ADVANCE:

Bake the cake layers, and set aside to cool and settle for 4–6 hours. Fill, stack and carve the cake into the
backpack shape. Cover the cake with ganache and allow the ganache to set overnight.

HIPPOS

1. Roll 45 g grey modelling paste into a smooth ball. Divide 5 g grey modelling paste into two equal pieces and shape into teardrops.

2. Shape the large ball into a calabash for the head. Press a bone tool into the wide end of each teardrop and then roll the edges towards each other to create ears.

3. Mark the eyes on the head with a toothpick and add eyelashes by pushing the edge of the toothpick from the eye outwards. Create large nostrils and a mouth on the side with the large end of a veining tool.

4. Attach the ears to the top of the head with edible glue.

5. Roll two tiny balls of black modelling paste and glue onto the eye markings. Create a smaller hippo with the remaining grey modelling paste.

GIRAFFE

1. Divide 50 g orange modelling paste into two equal balls for the neck and head, and divide 5 g orange modelling paste into two equal balls for the ears (see photo of steps 1–5 on opposite page).

2. Roll one of the large balls into a sausage about 10 cm long to create the neck. Insert a kebab stick into the centre of the sausage, allowing the stick to protrude about 3 cm at one end and about 7 cm at the other end.

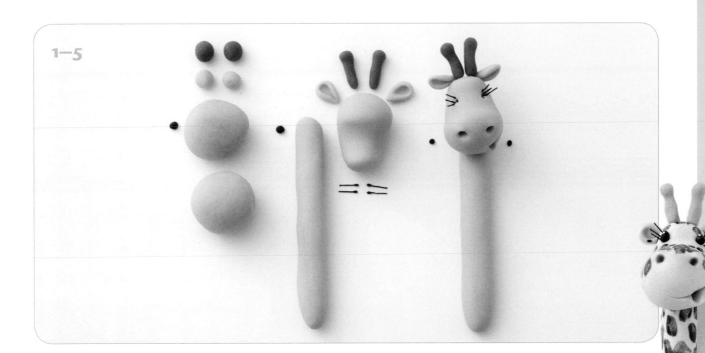

3. Roll the second large ball into a calabash. Shape the two smaller balls into teardrops and press the large end of a bone tool into the wider ends to create the ears. Roll the edges towards each other. Attach the ears to the sides of the head with a little edible glue.

4. Mark the eyes on the head with a toothpick and use the large end of the veining tool to create nostrils and a mouth. Press three black stamens into each eye to create lashes.

5. Shape 7 g brown modelling paste into two horns. Attach these to the top of the head between the ears with edible glue.

6. Roll two tiny balls of black modelling paste and glue onto the eye markings.

7. Stick the head onto the shorter piece of stick at the top of the neck with a little edible glue.

8. Paint giraffe markings with brown or ivory gel colour onto the face and neck. Allow to dry.

ZEBRAS

1. Roll 30 g white modelling paste into a smooth ball for the head and divide 5 g white modelling paste into two equal balls for the ears.

2. Shape the head into a calabash. Mark the eyes with a toothpick and the nostrils and mouth with a veining tool as for the giraffe and hippo.

3. Shape the ears in the same way as for the hippo and giraffe, pinching the top of each to form a point. Attach the ears to the side of the face with edible glue.

4. Press two black stamens into each eye to create lashes.

5. Roll two tiny balls of black modelling paste and glue onto the eye markings.

6. Draw markings on the zebra's head with a black edible ink marker. Repeat with the remaining white modelling paste to create a second zebra.

LIONS

1. Roll 25 g yellow modelling paste into a smooth ball for the head. Divide 6 g yellow modelling paste into two equal balls for the cheeks and 5 g yellow modelling paste into two equal balls for the ears.

2. Shape the head into a calabash and the ears as for the other animals.

3. Mark the eyes with a toothpick. Press the cheeks flat and attach to the face with edible glue. Mark with the tip of a toothpick. Create a mouth with a veining tool.

4. Add a small ball of light pink modelling paste for a nose.

5. Roll two tiny balls of black modelling paste and glue onto the eye markings.

6. Attach the ears to the side of the head with edible glue.

7. To create a mane, mix 20 g yellow modelling paste with a small amount of shortening. Press this through an extruder with a medium multi-hole disk to create hair. Attach the extruded paste around the edge of the head with edible glue. Model a lioness with the remaining yellow modelling paste, leaving off the mane.

MONKEY

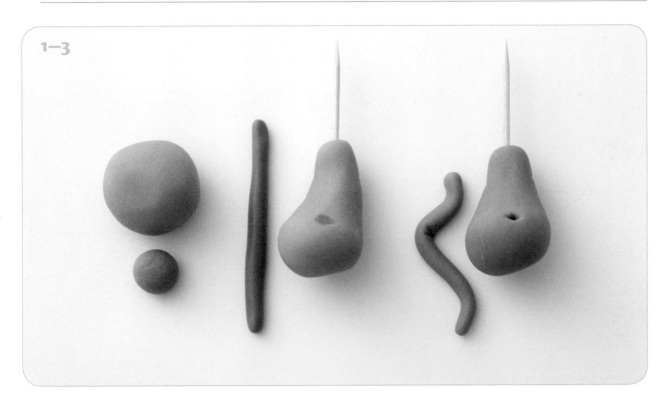

1—3

1. Roll 25 g brown modelling paste into a smooth ball for the body and 10 g brown modelling paste into a long, thin sausage for the tail.

2. Shape the body into a calabash and push a support stick for the head into the narrow end. Mark the belly button with a toothpick.

3. Shape the tail and attach to the body with edible glue.

4. Roll 15 g brown modelling paste into a smooth ball for the head and 8 g brown modelling paste into two teardrops for the ears (see overleaf).

5. Shape the head into a calabash and push in the narrow part to create a snout. Press a bone tool into the wide end of each ear to give it shape.

6. Mark the eyes with a toothpick, the nostrils and mouth with a veining tool and the centre of the snout with the back of a knife. Attach the ears to the sides of the head with edible glue. Roll two tiny balls of black modelling paste and glue onto the eye markings.

7. Divide 20 g brown modelling paste into four equal balls for the limbs.

4—6

8. Use the techniques on page 35 and 36 to create the arms and legs.

9. Attach the right arm and legs to the body with edible glue.

10. Attach the head and adjust the position to face out from the cake.

11. Create a tuft of hair from a little extruded brown paste and attach to the top of the head.

12. Model and attach the left arm only once the monkey is placed onto the cake to give the figure more movement.

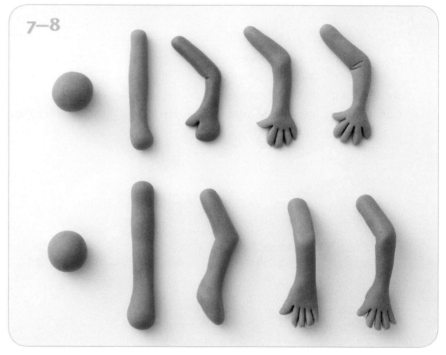

7—8

COVERING THE CAKE

1. Brush the ganached cake with clear alcohol or lemon juice. Roll out 800 g brown fondant and cover the cake. Smooth and tuck the edges of the fondant under the cake to create the bottom of the bag.

2. Press the tops of the three different sizes of drinking straws onto the surface of the fondant to create texture.

3. Mark the side joins of the bag with a knife. Create stitches with the tip of a toothpick or a quilting wheel tool.

4. Place the cake onto the prepared board.

5. Dust the fondant with brown dusting powder, emphasising the edges of the bag that would be most worn.

FRONT POCKET

1. Roll 80 g brown fondant to a thickness of 2 mm. Cut out the front pocket using the template on page 146. Mark the edges of the pocket with the tip of a toothpick to make stitches.
2. Mark five places on the front of the cake where each zebra, lion and giraffe will be attached. These should be 8 cm from the base of the cake. Stick 15 g excess brown fondant onto the front of the cake under each place marker. This will create the illusion of a body for each animal once the pocket is attached.
3. Attach the pocket to the cake with edible glue.

FLAP AND STRAPS

1. Roll out 300 g brown fondant to a thickness of 3 mm. Cut out the bag flap, handle and straps using the templates on page 146 and 147. Mark the stitching with the tip of a toothpick.
2. Cut out a 2 cm round hole from the bag flap as indicated on the template.
3. Attach the flap to the cake with edible glue.
4. Attach the handle to the top of the bag flap. Attach each strap at the top and bottom of the bag, draping the straps for a natural 'soft leather' look.
5. Model a toggle from 10 g brown modelling paste and attach over the hole.

ASSEMBLY

1. Paint glints in the animals' eyes by dipping a toothpick into ivory gel colour.
2. Roll out 75 g brown fondant in a rough circle to create a mud pond. Glue the pond to the board on the left of the bag.
3. For the grass, fill an icing bag with lime-green royal icing and attach a grass nozzle. Pipe grass around edge of the pond on the cake board. Sprinkle fondant sand around the edge of the mud pond and the bag.
4. Stick the hippo heads onto the mud pond with edible glue.
5. Insert a toothpick into the zebras' and lions' heads. Insert all the animals into the front pocket.
6. Stick the monkey onto the top of the cake and model the left arm to grab the bag handle.
7. Create a little dragonfly for embellishment. For the body, roll 5 g white modelling paste into a 3 cm sausage tapering one end. For the eyes, cut off the ball ends of two black stamens and push these into the thicker end of the body. Allow to dry.
8. Attach the wings (see page 90) half way along the body on both sides with edible glue. Attach the dragonfly to cake with edible glue.

First birthday cake

I love to make this cake for a child's first birthday; it is such a significant day to celebrate and is always much anticipated. This little mouse has beaten everyone to the tasting of the cake.

Recipes

- 2 quantities coconut sponge cake baked in three round cake tins (p. 20)
- ½ quantity orange buttercream (variations p. 21)
- 1 quantity white chocolate ganache (p. 23)
- ½ quantity royal icing (p. 25)

EQUIPMENT

large and small rolling pins
1 cm round cutter
2 cm round cutter
4 cm round cutter
toothpicks
primula blossom cutter
3 kebab sticks
green florist tape
florist wire
extruder
support stick
bone tool
sharp knife
large and small paintbrushes
veining tool
piping bag
icing tube

MATERIALS

30 cm round cake board
ribbon
900 g brown fondant
500 g white fondant
450 g light blue fondant
100 g dark blue fondant
80 g off-white modelling paste
45 g light blue modelling paste
30 g light pink modelling paste
25 g flame-red modelling paste
20 g white modelling paste
20 g dark blue modelling paste
15 g moss-green modelling paste
10 g yellow modelling paste
10 g dark brown modelling paste
3 white stamens
yellow dusting powder
orange dusting powder
ivory gel colour
non-toxic glue
edible glue
shortening
clear alcohol or lemon juice

Preparation

TWO DAYS OR UP TO A WEEK IN ADVANCE:
Make the candle, strawberry and mouse.
Cover the cake board (see below) and trim with ribbon.

ONE DAY IN ADVANCE:
Bake the cake layers, and allow to cool and settle for up to 6 hours. Fill and stack the cake. Allow to settle for
half an hour to an hour before sculpting the cake into a large slice of cake. Cover the entire cake in
ganache and allow the ganache to set overnight.

CAKE BOARD

1. Cover the cake board with 450 g light blue fondant.
2. With 1 cm and 2 cm round cutters, cut out and remove the circles with the tip of a toothpick.
3. Replace the removed fondant with brown, dark blue and white circles cut from rolled-out fondant.
4. Glue the ribbon around the edge with non-toxic glue. Set the board aside to dry.

STRAWBERRY

1. Roll 25 g flame-red modelling paste into a smooth ball. Roll out 15 g moss-green modelling paste and cut out a primula blossom. Roll a tiny stalk from the remaining moss-green paste and attach to the centre of the primula with edible glue.
2. Shape the strawberry and press the tip of a toothpick into the surface of the paste to create the pips on the outside.
3. Stick the primula blossom onto the top of the strawberry with edible glue.

CANDLE

1. Cut three kebab sticks to a length of 13 cm.
2. Wrap green florist tape tightly around the sticks and insert a 10 cm length of florist wire at one end. The wire should protrude at least 2 cm out of the bundle.
3. Mix some shortening with 20 g each of white, dark blue and light blue modelling paste. Extrude a 22 cm length of each colour. Lay the three colours side by side and wrap them around the bound bundle as shown. Leave 3 cm of stick bare at the base.
4. Shape 10 g yellow modelling paste into a flame shape. Dust the entire surface of the flame with yellow dusting powder. Dust the tip of the flame with orange dusting powder.

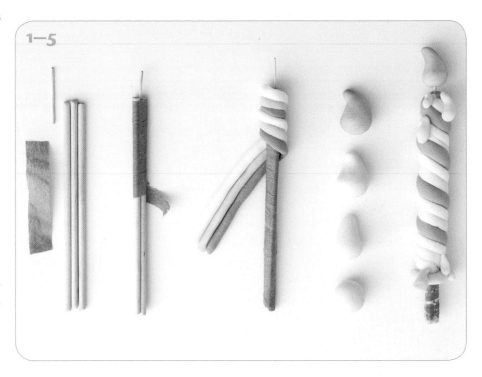

5. Push the flame onto the florist wire protruding from the candle and finish by attaching drips of wax made from the remaining light blue modelling paste.

MOUSE

1. Roll 40 g off-white modelling paste into a smooth ball for the body and shape 25 g off-white modelling paste into a teardrop for the head.
2. Shape the body as shown and mark the belly button with the tip of a toothpick. Insert a support stick for the head into the narrow end of the body.

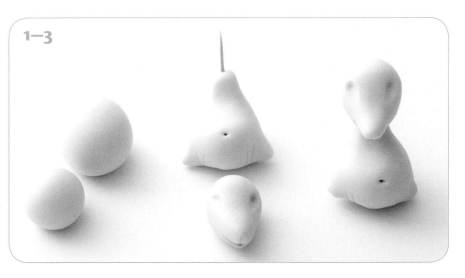

3. Press the small side of a bone tool into the sides of the head to create eye cavities and push the back of a knife into the narrow end to create a mouth. Stick the head onto the body.

4. Roll 25 g light blue modelling paste into a smooth ball for the jacket and divide and shape 10 g light blue modelling paste into two teardrops for the sleeves.

5. Roll out the ball to a thickness of 2 mm. Cut out a 4 cm circle and a jacket collar as shown. Push the back of a paintbrush into the wide ends of the sleeves to create hollows for the front paws.

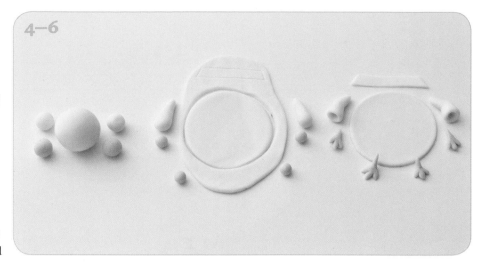

4–6

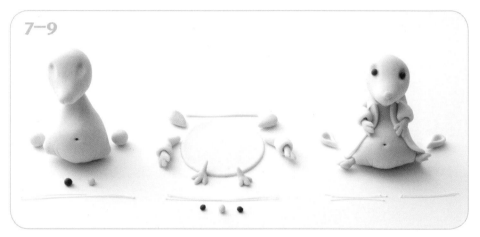

7–9

6. Create four paws from 20 g light pink modelling paste. Cut toes and fingers with a sharp knife and shape using your fingers.

7. Make a pair of ears with 8 g off-white modelling paste using the instructions on page 45, steps 8 and 9 of the tiny teddy.

8. Stick the front paws onto the ends of the sleeves with edible glue. Roll two tiny balls of dark brown modelling paste and glue onto the eye markings on the head. Roll a small ball of light pink modelling paste to form a nose and attach to the end of the snout.

9. Roll the 4 cm light blue circle from left to right to stretch it. Wrap this around the back of the mouse body to create a jacket, before attaching the collar and sleeves with edible glue. Stick the back paws onto the legs on the base of the body.

10. Cut three white stamens in half and push three into either side of the mouse head to create

whiskers. Brush a small amount of royal icing onto the whiskers to make the mouse look like he has just eaten some cake.

11. Paint a glint in each eye with toothpick dipped in ivory gel colour.

COVERING THE CAKE

1. Brush the ganached cake with clear alcohol or lemon juice.
2. Cover the cake in brown fondant rolled out to a thickness of 3 mm.
3. Mark the halfway point around the cake where the drippy icing will be attached.

DRIPPY ICING

1. To make the drippy icing, roll 80 g white fondant into four rough sausages. Twist each end of the sausages to create small knots. Attach the sausages to the cake along the marked line with edible glue. Use a veining tool to mark folds in the icing.
2. Place the cake onto the prepared cake board.
3. Attach additional drips down the side and along the bottom of the cake.
4. Roll out 400 g white fondant to a thickness of 4 mm. Drape the fondant over the top of the cake. Tuck the edges under themselves to create a thick puffy layer. Mark folds with a veining tool.

ASSEMBLY

1. Pipe a large rosette of royal icing onto the top of the cake. Place the strawberry in the centre of the rosette.
2. Push the candle into the top of the cake and add a few light blue wax drips to the base of the candle.
3. Dig a small amount of fondant from the front of the cake with a veining tool or toothpick.
4. Glue the mouse to rest against the cake and glue the fondant into its paws.
5. Add a few fondant crumbs to the board for the finishing touch.

Alternative first birthday cake

Cover the sculptured cake in pink fondant to create a first birthday cake
for a little girl. Make the candle in the same manner, substituting the blue and white
modelling paste with dark pink, light pink and apricot modelling paste.
Cover the board in light pink fondant. Cut out and remove small blossoms with a
blossom cutter and 1 cm circles with a circle cutter. Roll out 20 g each of apricot, dark
orange and dark pink fondant. Cut small blossoms from the apricot and dark orange
fondant and circles from the dark pink fondant. Replace the removed shapes with the
cut-outs and smooth the board with a fondant smoother.

Surf shack cake

This beach-themed cake is perfect for anyone who loves to spend their summers on the sand and in the sea.

Recipes

- 1½ quantities double chocolate cake baked in three 20 cm square cake tins (p. 18)
- 1 quantity vanilla buttercream (p. 21)
- 1 quantity dark chocolate ganache (p. 23)

EQUIPMENT

large and small rolling pins
sharp knife
fondant smoother
large and small paintbrushes
roof tile impression mat
templates for surfboards (p. 144)
baking paper
2 saucers
toothpicks
star cutters
scouring pad
shell tool

MATERIALS

25 cm square cake board
ribbon
1 kg turquoise fondant
550 g white fondant
400 g bright yellow fondant
50 g flame-red fondant
400 g white modelling paste
30 g orange modelling paste
40 g light brown modelling paste
9 g off-white modelling paste
4 g lime-green modelling paste
buttercup-yellow dusting powder
lime-green dusting powder
apricot dusting powder
orange dusting powder
black edible ink marker
clear alcohol or lemon juice
cornflour
non-toxic glue
edible glue
125 ml brown sugar

Preparation

UP TO A WEEK IN ADVANCE:

Cover the board in 550 g white fondant and glue the ribbon to the edges with non-toxic glue.
Make the surfboards, sandals, starfish, shells and stones.

ONE DAY IN ADVANCE:

Bake the cake layers, and allow to cool and settle. Fill, stack, sculpt and ganache the cake.

SCULPTING AND COVERING THE CAKE

1. Carve a topsy-turvy cake using the techniques on page 27. Carve a slanted top.
2. Ganache the cake, making the edges as sharp as possible. Allow the ganache to set.
3. Roll out 250 g turquoise fondant to a thickness of 3 mm.
4. Brush the ganached cake with clear alcohol or lemon juice.
5. Lay the left side of the cake on the rolled-out fondant. Trim around the cake. Pull away the excess fondant and tip the cake back to an upright position. Smooth the fondant with a fondant smoother. Repeat with the right, rear and finally the front of the cake.
6. Mark the fondant to look like panels of wood with a sharp knife. Push the end of a small paintbrush into the corner of each panel to create nail marks.

ROOF

1. Roll out 400 g bright yellow fondant to a thickness of 3 mm.
2. Press a roof tile impression mat firmly and evenly into the fondant.
3. Measure the top of the cake and cut the fondant a little bigger.
4. Drape over the top of the shack.

SURFBOARDS

1. Trace the surfboard templates on page 144 onto baking paper. Cut out each board.
2. Roll out 200 g white modelling paste to a thickness of 5 mm. Lay the cut-out templates onto the paste and cut around them with a sharp knife.
3. Draw the back of a knife down the centre of each surfboard.
4. Rest each surfboard on a saucer dusted with cornflour and leave overnight to dry.
5. Dust each dry surfboard with dusting powder, dusting the entire board with the lightest colour first, then with a deeper shade over the bottom half of the board and finally with the deepest shade on the base of the board.
6. Decorate the surfboards with surf logos, etc. using a black edible ink marker.

STARFISH

1. Roll out 30 g orange modelling paste to a thickness of 5 mm.

2. Cut out star shapes with star cutters.
3. Mark the starfish with the tip of a toothpick.

SHELLS

1. Roll 3 g off-white modelling paste into a teardrop and place onto a flat work surface.

2. Press the grooved part of a shell tool onto the paste to form a shell.

SANDALS

1. Shape 2 g lime-green modelling paste into a ball.
2. Place your forefinger in the centre of the ball and roll into a dog-bone shape in the palm of your hand.
3. Flatten the bone on a work surface and work into a sandal shape. Texture the sandal with a texture mat or clean scouring pad.

4. Roll a small amount of yellow modelling paste into a thin sausage. Pinch halfway along into a V-shape.
5. Glue the V onto the top half of the sandal to finish. Make a second sandal.

TOWELS

1. Roll out 30 g white modelling paste to a thickness of 1 mm.
2. Decorate by sticking stripes of rolled-out coloured modelling paste onto the white.

3. Press a scouring pad down firmly onto the rolled-out paste. This will give a texture similar to towelling.
4. Cut two rectangles 10 x 5 cm. Roll up one towel and keep the other to drape from the roof of the shack.

ASSEMBLY

1. Place the covered cake onto the covered cake board. Secure it with a little ganache or buttercream.
2. Roll out and cut a door from 40 g flame-red fondant. Mark the fondant to look like panels of wood and attach a small doorknob.
3. Secure the door to the front of the cake with edible glue.

4. Brush the cake board with edible glue and spoon brown sugar over the surface of the board to create sand.
5. Drape one towel from the roof, roll stones from light brown modelling paste and place one on the towel. Rest the surfboards against the shack and add the shells, starfish, sandals and rolled-up towel to finish.

Pillow cake

This pillow cake will wow your guests, but is surprisingly easy to sculpt and cover. Adding a tiny fairy princess perched on top of the pillow will give it that extra something special.

Recipes

- ½ quantity double chocolate cake baked in two 15 cm square cake tins (p. 18)
- 1 quantity dark or white chocolate ganache (p. 23)
- ½ quantity chocolate buttercream (variations p. 21)

EQUIPMENT

large and small rolling pins
sharp knife
large and small paintbrushes
bone tool
toothpicks
templates for pillow and princess skirt (p. 144 and 145)
baking paper
large carnation cutter
2 cm round cutter
1.5 cm round cutter
extruder
serrated knife
fondant smoother
veining tool
multi-hole disk extruder
20 sewing pins
small star cutter
small five-petal blossom cutter
star paper punch
filigree edge paper punch

MATERIALS

30 cm round cake board
ribbon
600 g light blue fondant
500 g white fondant
155 g lilac modelling paste
60 g flesh-toned modelling paste
60 g light blue modelling paste
50 g dark brown modelling paste
50 g white modelling paste
5 g black modelling paste
lilac dusting powder
pale pink edible glitter
brown gel colour
white gel colour
unbreakable lace in white (p. 36)
blue dragées
shortening
edible glue
non-toxic glue
clear alcohol or lemon juice

Preparation

UP TO A WEEK IN ADVANCE:
Cover the cake board.
Make the fairy wings (see recipe for unbreakable lace on page 36), fairy princess, wand and tiara.

ONE DAY IN ADVANCE:
Bake the cake layers, and allow to cool and settle. Fill, stack and sculpt the cake and cover with ganache.

CAKE BOARD

1. Roll out 600 g light blue fondant to a thickness of 2 mm.
2. Drape the fondant over the cake board, creating folds to resemble a piece of fabric. Trim excess fondant with a sharp knife.
3. Gently lift the edges of the fondant and glue to the cake board with edible glue.
4. When the fondant is dry, dust it with lilac dusting powder.
5. Attach the ribbon with non-toxic glue.

1—5

1. Roll 20 g light blue modelling paste into a smooth ball for the body. Shape 5 g flesh-toned modelling paste into a teardrop for the neck.

2. Shape the ball into a fat sausage.

3. To create the fairy's waist, narrow the middle of the shape, leaving each side wider than the middle.

4. Cut out a V-shape from the top to create a space to add the neck.

5. Glue the neck into the V-shaped cut-out and press a dent into the base of the throat with the back of a bone tool.

6. Model two legs from 15 g flesh-toned modelling paste using the technique on page 36. Glue the legs together at the top of the thighs and model them in a sitting position. Glue the body to the top of the legs, moulding the base of the body around the legs. Insert a toothpick into the neck, pushing the support down the length of the body.

7

7. Roll 30 g white modelling paste to a thickness of 2 mm. Cut out two large carnation flowers. Frill the edges of each flower with a toothpick. Cut out the centre of each flower with a round cutter and cut through the remaining frill to lengthen it.

8. Roll 30 g light blue modelling paste to a thickness of 1 mm. Cut out a skirt using the princess skirt template on page 145 and two 2 cm circles. Wrap the skirt around the body, tucking it under the princess's bottom, and secure with edible glue. Mark darts with a sharp knife and attach the white frill to the bottom (see overleaf).

9. Mix a little shortening with 20 g lilac modelling paste. Extrude a narrow ribbon from an extruder. Glue the ribbon along the edge of the skirt, neckline and along the join at the top. Impress a pattern into the lilac trim with the tip of a toothpick.

10. Model two arms from 18 g flesh-toned modelling paste using the technique on page 35. Position and attach each arm to the shoulders of the body with a little edible glue and attach one 2 cm light blue circle over each shoulder to make a sleeve.

11. Make the face with 15 g flesh-toned modelling paste using the technique on page 34.

12. Attach the head to the body.

13. Make the hair from dark brown modelling paste and attach to the head.

14. Add a tiny blossom to the centre of her collar to finish.

TIARA

1. Roll 10 g white modelling paste to a thickness of less than 1 mm. Allow the paste to dry for about 5 minutes.

2. Gently slip the rolled-out paste into the slot of a filigree edge paper punch and press the punch down firmly.

3. Remove the paste cut-out carefully from the punch and trim to form the tiara. Shape over the handle of a wooden spoon.

4. Attach to the fairy princess with a little edible glue.

WAND

1. Roll 10 g white modelling paste to a thickness of less than 1mm. Allow the paste to dry for about 5 minutes.

2. Gently slip the rolled-out paste into the slot of a star paper punch and press the punch down firmly.

3. Remove the star carefully from the punch by tapping the punch on the work surface.

4. Roll 5 g lilac modelling paste into a thin sausage about 1 mm thick. Cut to a length of 4 cm.

5. Glue the star onto one end of the sausage. Dab a small amount of glue onto the star before dusting it with edible glitter.

SCULPTING THE PILLOW

1. Fill and stack the cake layers. Allow the filling to settle and firm up.
2. Trace the pillow template on page 144 onto baking paper and cut out.
3. Place the template on top of the cake and cut out the shape with a serrated knife.
4. Shape the pillow by cutting away the edges of the cake to give it a stuffed look. Flip over the cake and repeat on the underside.
5. Cover the top of the carved cake in ganache and allow to set for 5 minutes before flipping and covering the underside. Smooth the ganache to finish. Allow to set overnight or for an hour in the fridge.

COVERING THE PILLOW

1. Roll out 250 g white fondant to a thickness of 3 mm. Cut out a square from the fondant measuring 18 x 18 cm.
2. Brush the top of the ganached cake with clear alcohol or lemon juice.
3. Drape the square of fondant over the cake. Smooth it down the sides and into the corners.
4. Carefully flip over the cake onto the prepared board.
5. Roll out and cut a second square of white fondant as before. Drape this square over the exposed cake and smooth over with a fondant smoother. The edges of the two fondant squares should overlap slightly.
6. Trim the edges along the middle of each side with a sharp knife, removing the excess fondant.
7. Mark folds on the base of the cake where it will sit on the board with a veining tool.

QUILTING THE TOP OF THE PILLOW

1. While the fondant is still soft or flexible, score a crosshatch design on top with the back of a knife. Work from the top left corner to the bottom right corner.
2. Where each line crosses, mark a fold with a veining tool to form a fabric crease.
3. Use a dot of edible glue to stick a blue dragée where each line crosses.

ROPING

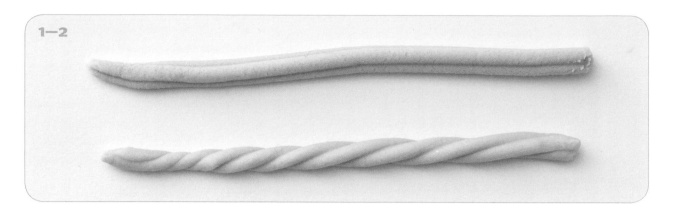

1—2

1. Mix a little shortening with the remaining lilac modelling paste and extrude a 16 cm length from an extruder.
2. Twist the length to create the roping.
3. Along the join of the top and bottom fondant squares, push five pins along each side, spacing them out evenly. Brush edible glue along the fondant joins on the cake (see opposite page).
4. Drape the roping on the pins and gently push to stick it along the join. Trim the rope at each corner as shown. Repeat for each of the four sides.

TASSELS

1. Extrude eight 5 cm lengths of lilac modelling paste mixed with shortening through a medium multi-hole extruder disk.
2. Slightly pinch the ends of one side together and attach one tassel to each of the four corners of the pillow with edible glue.
3. Pinch both ends of each of the remaining extruded lengths together.
4. Tuck the pinched ends under each other to create a 'knot'.
5. Attach one knot to each corner of the pillow with edible glue, covering the join of the tassel to the pillow.

TO FINISH

1. Glue the fairy princess to the top of the pillow cake. Attach her wings and add the wand and tiara.
2. Roll out the leftover light blue fondant to a thickness of 1 mm and cut narrow ribbons to drape onto the fabric of the board for interest.
3. Dust with a light sprinkling of pale pink edible glitter to add to the magical/enchanted quality of the cake.

3

4

Teddy bear cake

When I was a child, I loved to imagine that my stuffed animals got up to mischief while I was sleeping. These two bears have been caught unwrapping a gift and look terribly guilty. This is a lovely cake for a christening or naming ceremony or for a small child's birthday.

Recipes

- 1½ quantities double chocolate cake baked in three 15 cm square cake tins (p. 18)
- 1 quantity chocolate buttercream (variations p. 21)
- 1 quantity dark chocolate ganache (p. 23)

EQUIPMENT

large and small rolling pins

fondant smoother

sharp knife

large and small paintbrushes

Styrofoam cake dummy

toothpicks

support sticks

quilting tool

veining tool

bone tool

pizza cutter

ruler

MATERIALS

35 cm round cake board

ribbon

900 g butter-yellow fondant

550 g light blue fondant

400 g moss-green fondant

100 g white fondant

400 g light brown modelling paste

100 g dark brown modelling paste

20 g moss-green modelling paste

turquoise lustre dust

brown dusting powder

edible glue

non-toxic glue

clear alcohol or lemon juice

Preparation

Cover the cake board.

Make two teddy bears, shaping one on a Styrofoam cake dummy to look like he is climbing onto the cake.
Make the second bear sitting up.

ONE DAY IN ADVANCE:

Bake the cake layers, and allow to cool and settle. Level, fill and stack the cakes. Trim to make a cube.
Cover the cake with ganache and set aside for the ganache to set.

COVERING THE CAKE BOARD

1. Roll out 550 g light blue fondant to a thickness of 2–3 mm. Brush the cake board with water or edible glue.
2. Drape the fondant over the board and smooth with a fondant smoother. Trim excess fondant with a sharp knife.
3. Run the back of a knife along the fondant to create wood panels. Push the end of a small paintbrush handle into the corner of each panel to make nail marks. Create a wood-grain effect and dust the board with turquoise lustre dust.
4. Stick the ribbon along the edge of the board with non-toxic glue. Set aside to dry.

TEDDY BEARS

1. Roll 80 g light brown modelling paste into a smooth ball for the belly. Divide 20 g and 30 g light brown modelling paste into two equal balls for the arms and legs respectively.
2. Shape the belly into a calabash and push a support stick into the narrow end.
3. Mark a belly button with the tip of a toothpick and mark folds in the belly with the back of a knife.
4. Shape the arms and legs and attach them to either side of the belly with edible glue, tucking the tops of the legs around the back of the teddy. Mark stitching along the midline of the belly with the tip of a toothpick or a quilting tool.
5. Roll 60 g light brown paste into a smooth ball for the head. Shape 5 g light brown paste into two teardrops for the ears, pressing a bone tool into the wide end of each.
6. Shape the head into a calabash. Push the narrower end flat against the wider end to create a muzzle.

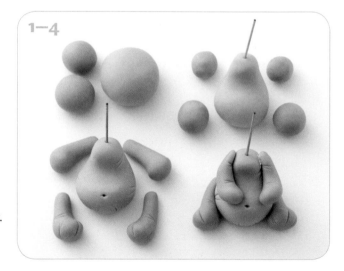

7. Mark the eyes with a toothpick and create stitches between them with a toothpick or quilting tool. Make the mouth by pushing the large end of a veining tool into the muzzle and pulling down to widen it. Push the back of a knife from the tip of the muzzle to the mouth.

8. Shape 5 g dark brown paste into an oval and attach to the top of the muzzle with edible glue. Attach the ears to the side of the head and two tiny balls of dark brown paste onto the eye markings.

9. Stick the head onto the belly and add patches of rolled-out moss-green modelling paste to the face and belly.

10. Roll 10 g dark brown modelling paste into four small balls.

11. Flatten them to make buttons and pierce each with two holes as shown.

12. Stick the buttons onto the joins of each arm and leg.

13. Dust the bear with brown dusting powder to finish.

14. Make a second bear lying on his belly and add a small tail. Shape and attach the left leg once the cake is assembled to give the impression that the bear is climbing up the cake.

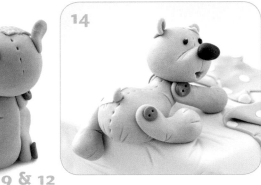

RIBBON

1. Roll out 400 g moss-green fondant to a thickness of 1 mm.
2. Roll small balls of white fondant and place them randomly on top.
3. Press firmly down on the white balls with a fondant smoother until they are flush with the rolled-out fondant to make a polka dot pattern.
4. Use a pizza cutter to cut out four strips 5 cm wide and 25–30 cm long.
5. Roll up two strips and use the other two for the sides of the gift cake.
6. Cut a V-shape in the ends of each ribbon.

ASSEMBLY

1. Brush the filled, stacked and ganached cube cake with clear alcohol or lemon juice.
2. Roll out 900 g butter-yellow fondant to a thickness of 3 mm.
3. Cover the cube with fondant and smooth the edges with a fondant smoother. Trim excess fondant and carefully neaten the edges of the cake with a sharp knife.
4. Transfer the covered cake to the prepared board.
5. Use the edge of a ruler to mark the fold lines on the sides of the cube.
6. Stick the long strips of ribbon onto the centre of the front and right side of the cube. Drape the ends of the ribbons to look like they are about to fall off the cake.
7. Place the rolled up strips on the cake as shown.
8. Place one bear sitting in front of the parcel and the second bear on top, attaching the left leg once he is in position.
9. Mark around the feet and arms of the top bear to look like the paper is wrinkling.

Alternative teddy bear cake

Change the colour of the fondant covering the gift cake to light pink and colour the fondant for the ribbon apricot. The fondant covering the board can be changed to a soft butter-yellow to make this cake more girly. You could also scatter a few blossoms on the cake board or even place one in the sitting bear's paw.

Circus cake

The circus never fails to thrill children of all ages and the clowns are always the stars of any circus act.

Recipes

- 1 quantity vanilla bean sponge baked in three 15 cm round cake tins (p. 19)
- ½ quantity vanilla buttercream (p. 21)
- ½ quantity white chocolate ganache (p. 23)

EQUIPMENT

large and small rolling pins
cobblestone impression mat
sharp knife
large and small paintbrushes
fondant smoother
Styrofoam cake dummy
extruder
bone tool
star cutter
five-petal blossom cutter
toothpicks
frilling tool
piping tube
circle cutter
veining tool
support sticks
6 cm round cutter
3 cm round cutter
24-gauge florist wire
3 kebab sticks

MATERIALS

35 cm round cake board
ribbon
1.2 kg white fondant
200 g flame-red fondant
50 g black fondant
150 g flame-red modelling paste
150 g orange modelling paste
100 g yellow modelling paste
100 g lime-green modelling paste
100 g turquoise modelling paste
100 g brown modelling paste
60 g white modelling paste
10 g black modelling paste
brown dusting powder
edible glitter
non-toxic glue
edible glue
shortening
clear alcohol or lemon juice

Preparation

UP TO A WEEK IN ADVANCE:

Cover the cake board in 600 g white fondant. Press the cobblestone impression mat firmly onto the fondant. Trim excess fondant from the board. Dust the cobblestones with brown dusting powder using a large brush. Set aside to dry.

Make two clowns, one sitting with legs spread wide and the other lying on his tummy.

Make the tent poles, sticking them into a Styrofoam cake dummy to dry.

ONE DAY IN ADVANCE:

Bake the cake layers, and allow to cool and settle for at least 6 hours. Fill, stack, sculpt and cover the cake with ganache. Leave overnight to allow the ganache to set.

TENT POLES

1. Mix a little shortening with 40 g flame-red and 40 g orange modelling paste.

2. Extrude a straight length of each colour. Lay the extruded colours next to each other.

3. Twist the colours around a kebab stick to cover the stick in alternating colours. Leave the bottom 1 cm and the top 3 cm of the stick empty of paste. Make two tent poles.

CLOWNS

1. For the trousers, divide 30 g turquoise modelling paste into two equal balls. For the shoes, divide 24 g orange modelling paste into two equal balls.

2. Roll each turquoise ball into a thick sausage, slightly narrowing one end. Bend each sausage halfway to form knees and mark folds in the trousers with the back of a knife. Shape the shoes as shown and mark the soles with a knife blade.

3. Open the wide end of each trouser leg with a bone tool. Glue the trouser legs in a V-shape with the narrow ends touching. Roll out a ball of flame-red modelling paste and cut out a tiny square patch. Glue the patch to the side of one shoe and mark large stitches with the back of a knife.

4. For the body, roll 20 g lime-green modelling paste into a smooth ball and then into a cone. Divide 20 g

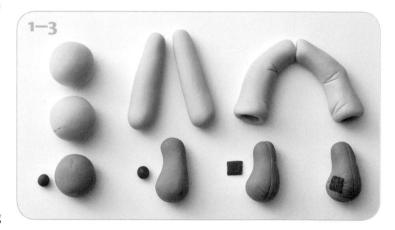

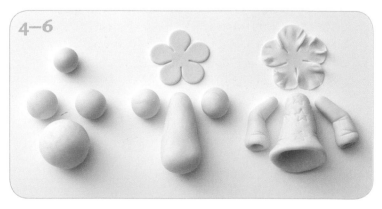

lime-green modelling paste into two equal balls and shape each into a cone to form the sleeves.

5. Roll out yellow modelling paste until very thin and cut out three five-petal blossoms. Frill each petal with a toothpick or frilling tool. These will become the collar of the clown's shirt.

6. With a bone tool and your fingers, hollow out the wider end of the body into a bell shape. Mark folds in the shirt fabric with the back of a knife and emboss stars onto it with a star cutter. Bend the sleeves at the elbows and mark the fabric folds as for the legs. Hollow the wide end of each sleeve to accommodate the hands. Attach each sleeve to the body with edible glue.

7. For the face, roll 20 g white modelling paste into a ball.

8. Flatten and shape one end so that it is slightly narrower. Mark the eyes with the tip of a toothpick.

9. Roll 5 g flame-red modelling paste into a short sausage and form into a crescent. Push one half of a circle cutter or piping tube into the crescent to form a grin. Open the mouth with a veining tool and mark dimples with the tip of a toothpick.

10. For the nose, glue a ball of flame-red modelling paste to the centre of the face. Stick the mouth under the nose with edible glue. Roll two tiny balls of black paste for eyes and attach with edible glue.

11. To make a gloved hand, roll 5 g white modelling paste into a smooth ball.

12. Shape into a skittle and flatten the wider end.

13. Cut a thumb, bending it back slightly.

14. Cut four fingers and shape and neaten by working each between your thumb and forefinger.

15. Mark seam details with a knife and the tip of a toothpick. Make a second glove with the thumb on the opposite side.

16. To assemble, stick the shirt body on top of the trouser legs. Push a support stick into the body from the top to support the head.

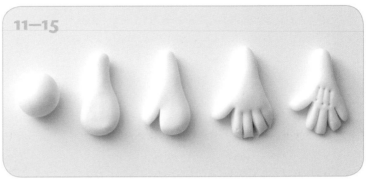

17. Thread and glue each frilled collar onto the shoulders and attach the head, pushing it down onto the support stick.

18. Extrude some orange modelling paste mixed with shortening through the multi-holed disk of an extruder and glue to the sides of the clown's face.

19. Attach each gloved hand into a hollowed-out sleeve.

20. Add a patch to one trouser leg and highlight each star on the shirt with edible glitter.

21. Create a second clown using different colours and position him on his belly. Add a hat with flower detail.

1. Fill and stack the cake layers. Carve the cake into the tent shape using the picture as a guide. Cover the cake in ganache, place on a board and allow to set overnight.

2. Brush the ganached cake with clear alcohol or lemon juice.

3. Roll out 50 g black fondant and stick onto the front of the sculpted cake where the tent opening will be. Mark the board with a dot of royal icing where the centre of the black fondant is on the cake.

4. Cover the entire cake in white fondant rolled out to a thickness of 3 mm. Smooth the edges and trim excess fondant with a sharp knife.

5. Cut an opening for the tent in the centre of where the black fondant is positioned underneath the white fondant. Roll back the white fondant to reveal the black underneath. Mark the folds in the fabric with the large end of a veining tool.

6. Roll out 150 g flame-red fondant to a thickness of 3 mm and cut strips about 1.5 cm wide. Lay the strips over the white fondant in a striped pattern running down the length of the cake.

7. Cut a 6 cm circle from rolled-out flame-red fondant with a scone cutter. Glue this over the joins at the top of the cake. Roll a ball of red fondant, squash it slightly and place it on top of the circle. Use a knife to make fabric creases in it.

8. Insert a kebab stick down the centre of the tent, allowing it to protrude 3 cm above the cake.

9. Cut eight 3 cm white circles and 10 flame-red circles from rolled-out fondant. Trim the tops from each circle as shown below and use to trim the edge of the tent.

10. Extrude a thin rope of flame-red modelling paste mixed with shortening and stick this along the flat top of trimming to finish off the tent.

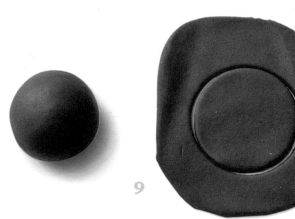

ASSEMBLY

1. Transfer the cake to the cake board, positioning it with enough room for the clowns to sit and lie in front of the tent.

2. Wrap two lengths of florist wire around the kebab stick protruding out of the top of the tent. Pull one to each side of the cake. Allow 17 cm of wire to remain clear and wrap the remaining wire around the top of each prepared tent pole. Rest the base of each tent pole on the board, leaning them at an angle.

3. Roll brown modelling paste into a collection of stone shapes and stick these around the base of each tent pole to secure them to the board.

4. Cut triangles from rolled-out turquoise and yellow modelling paste. Paint edible glue onto the base of each triangle and fold them over the wire to create the bunting.

5. Roll 10 g brown modelling paste into a thick sausage. Pinch one end to make a ball. Create a wood texture with the blade of a knife. Brush the top of the kebab stick in the top of the cake with edible glue and push the brown paste down over the stick to cover the wire wrapped around it. Repeat this for the tops of each tent pole with 15 g brown paste.

6. Roll out 20 g yellow modelling paste into a rectangle measuring 7 cm x 4 cm. Mark it with wood grain and press the end of a paintbrush handle into each corner. Stick the rectangle above the tent door using edible glue.

7. Glue both clowns in front of the tent and glue a ribbon around the board edge with non-toxic glue to finish it off.

Toadstool cake

My daughter's favourite bedtime stories always involve fairies that live at the bottom of our garden. In every story I include fairies with her and her best friends' names, making them the heroes of each story. This cake brings these stories to life. Even without the tiny fairies, it will enchant any little girl.

Recipes

- 4 quantities vanilla bean sponge baked in five 20 cm cake tins (p. 19)
- 1 quantity vanilla buttercream (p. 21)
- 2 quantities white chocolate ganache (p. 23)
- 1 quantity royal icing (tint half dark moss-green and half light moss-green) (p. 25)

EQUIPMENT

large and small rolling pins
scouring pad
sharp knife
fondant smoother
bone tool
small daisy plunger cutter
five-petal blossom cutter
primula blossom cutter
medium carnation cutter
five-petal blossom veiner
5 cm round cutter
template for door (p. 144)
baking paper
toothpicks
spirit level
25 cm dinner plate
4 dowels (cut to height of bottom tier)
kebab stick
large and small paintbrushes
icing bag
grass tube

MATERIALS

round cake board
15 cm round cake board
ribbon
1 kg white fondant
500 g lime-green fondant
500 g flame-red fondant
150 g white modelling paste
150 g light brown modelling paste
150 g brown modelling paste
50 g dark brown modelling paste
50 g moss-green modelling paste
50 g light blue modelling paste
50 g pink modelling paste
brown dusting powder
pearl lustre dust
white gel colour
15 tiny pearl dragées
materials for 2 fairies (p. 56 and 57)
materials for 5 toadstools (p. 55)
non-toxic glue
edible glue
clear alcohol or lemon juice
10 ml fondant sand (p. 32)

Preparation

UP TO A WEEK IN ADVANCE:

Cover the large cake board in 500 g lime-green fondant. Use a scouring pad to texture the edge of the board.
Set aside to dry. Glue the ribbon to the edge of the board with non-toxic glue.
Make the fairies, blossoms and chimney.

ONE DAY IN ADVANCE:

Bake the cake layers, and allow to cool and settle for at least 6 hours. Level, fill and stack three layers. Level, fill
and stack the remaining two layers, thereby making two cakes for the different parts of the toadstool. Carve the
cakes and cover both in white chocolate ganache.

FAIRIES

1. Use the technique on pages 56 and 57 to create two tiny fairies.

2. Roll out 50 g light brown modelling paste and roll into a log for the fairies to sit on.

CHIMNEY

1. Roll 80 g brown modelling paste into a ball.
2. Place the ball on a work surface and press firmly down on the top with a fondant smoother to flatten the two ends. Hollow out one flattened side with your thumb and forefinger and pinch the edges to a consistent thickness.

3. Make wood-grain texture around the outside of the chimney with a knife. Make a hole in the wood by pushing the bone tool into the side of the chimney.

FLOWER POTS

1. Shape 10 g brown modelling paste into a walnut. Hollow out one side of the walnut with a bone tool and mark the exterior with the blade of a knife to add texture.
2. Thinly roll out a little moss-green and light blue modelling paste. Cut five small daisies from the moss-green paste and three tiny blossoms from the light blue paste.

3. Stick the green daisies on top of the pot to create leaves. Press the blue blossoms into a flower veiner, dust the centres with pearl lustre dust and stick a tiny pearl dragée into the centre of each.

4. Glue the blossoms on top of the leaves. Make four full pots and one that will be positioned to look as if it has toppled over.

BLOSSOMS

Make six light blue, six pink and six white blossoms using the technique on page 33.

SMALL TOADSTOOLS

Make five tiny toadstools using the technique on page 55.

WINDOWS

1. Roll three balls of brown modelling paste, 10 g, 5 g and 5 g.
2. Roll the large ball into a 12 cm-long sausage and the two smaller balls into 4 cm-long sausages. Mark each with wood grain.
3. Glue the ends of the long sausage together to create a circle. Glue the short sausages together to form a cross. Flatten the ends of each cross and dab with a little edible glue. Place the circle on top of the cross, pressing down gently where the paste touches.
4. Thinly roll out a little white modelling paste.
5. Cut out a 5 cm circle.
6. Mark a crosshatch pattern on the paste with the back of a knife and dust with pearl lustre dust.
7. Glue the window frame on top of the white window pane with edible glue. Make a second window, adding a tiny latch to each frame.

DOOR

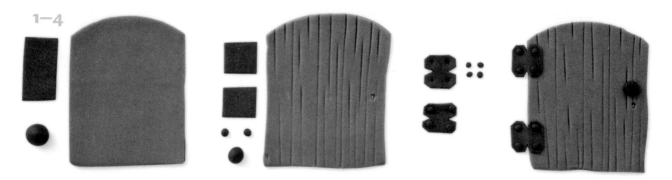

1—4

1. Roll out 40 g light brown modelling paste and cut out a door using the door template on page 144. Cut a 4 x 1 cm rectangle from rolled-out dark brown modelling paste, and cut into two squares.
2. Mark the wood panels on the door with the blade of a knife and mark a keyhole with the tip of a toothpick.
3. Shape the dark brown squares into hinges using the picture as a guide. Roll tiny balls of dark brown paste to make nails and glue into place on the hinges.
4. Glue the hinges onto the door with edible glue. Roll a small ball of dark brown paste for the doorknob and glue in place above the keyhole.
5. Make the rose leaf using the techinique on page 46 and attach to the front of the door with edible glue.

SCULPTING THE CAKES

1. For the base, level three layers of cake. Fill and stack the layers, allowing the buttercream to settle for 10 minutes before carving the cake into the base of the toadstool.
2. Cut the top of the cake straight across and use a spirit level to make sure that it is exactly level. This will ensure that the second tier will not topple over once it has been placed on top of the base.
3. For the top, level the remaining two cake layers. Fill and stack the layers. Carve the cake into an oval shape. Place this cake onto a 15 cm round cake board. Use a small amount of ganache to secure it to the board.
4. Shape a 100 g ball of white modelling paste into a cap to place on top of the top tier to add shape to the toadstool.
5. Cover both cakes in white chocolate ganache.

1—4

COVERING THE CAKES

1. Brush both ganached cakes with clear alcohol or lemon juice.
2. Roll out 700 g white fondant to a thickness of 2 mm. Cover the base cake and smooth with a fondant smoother. Trim excess fondant. Use a spirit level to check that the top of the cake is level. Transfer the cake to the prepared cake board.
3. Roll out 500 g flame-red fondant to a thickness of 2 mm. Cover the top cake and smooth with a fondant smoother. Trim excess fondant.

4. Roll out 300 g white fondant to a thickness of 2 mm. Cut a 25 cm circle using a dinner plate as a template. Brush the surface of the fondant circle with edible glue and place the 15 cm cake board with the top cake onto the circle.
5. Gently wrap the white fondant around the cake board and around the base of the top cake, smoothing with a fondant smoother.

ASSEMBLY

1. Insert four dowels into the base cake, allowing them to protrude 2 mm above the cake.
2. Place the top cake on top of the base cake, securing with a small amount of royal icing.
3. Use a kebab stick to create the fluted texture that is found on the underside of a toadstool.
4. Paint tiny dots of white gel colour onto the flame-red fondant of the top cake with the handle of a paintbrush or kebab stick.
5. Roll small balls of light brown modelling paste and push into the cake board to create a pathway to the front of the cake.
6. Dust the base of the toadstool with brown dusting powder.
7. Attach the chimney to the roof of the toadstool with a little royal icing.
8. Glue the door to the front of the cake with edible glue.
9. Attach a window on either side of the door. Roll 20 g white modelling paste to form the windowsills under each window. Brush each sill with brown dusting powder.
10. For the wooden door bell hook, roll 5 g of brown fondant into a sausage and mark it with wood grain. Bend slightly and attach to the toadstool with edible glue. For the bell, attach a flower (see page 33) to the bottom of the wooden hook.

11. Add the fairies sitting on the log and the flower pots, and arrange the flowers and toadstools around the board to create a garden.
12. Fill an icing bag with the two different shades of moss-green royal icing. Fit a grass tube and pipe grass around the base of the toadstool and along the pathway.
13. Sprinkle fondant sand around the base of each flower pot to add a finishing touch.

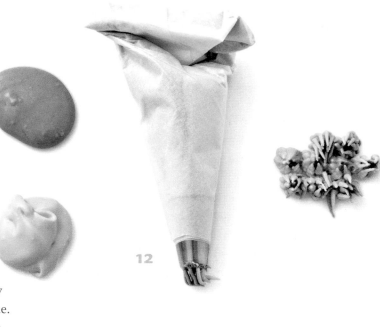

12

Golf cake

Although the design is quite simple, the shape of this cake mirrors the shape of a golf tee so well that it makes a lovely cake for a serious (or not so serious) golfer.

Recipes

- 1½ quantities double chocolate cake baked in three 20 cm square cake tins (p. 18)
- 1 quantity dark chocolate ganache (p. 23)
- 1 quantity chocolate buttercream (variations p. 21)
- 1 quantity royal icing (tint half lime-green) (p. 25)

EQUIPMENT

large and small rolling pins

sharp knife

1 large and 2 small paintbrushes

extra-long toothpick

piping bag

number 2 tube

icing bag

grass tube

template for argyle print (p. 144)

MATERIALS

25 cm square cake board

ribbon

1.2 kg light blue fondant

500 g lime-green fondant

200 g black fondant

60 g white modelling paste

20 g lime-green modelling paste

deep blue dusting powder

non-toxic glue

edible glue

clear alcohol or lemon juice

Preparation

UP TO A WEEK IN ADVANCE:
Cover the cake board in lime-green fondant. Attach the ribbon to the board with non-toxic glue. Make the golf tee and golf ball.

ONE DAY IN ADVANCE:
Bake the cake layers, and allow to cool and settle for at least 6 hours.
Fill and stack the cake, allowing the filling to settle before carving the cake into a square topsy-turvy shape (see page 27) and covering in ganache. The cake should stand overnight to allow the ganache to set.

GOLF BALL

1. Roll 60 g white modelling paste into a smooth ball.
2. Push the ball onto the handle of a paintbrush.
3. Make small dimples over the surface of the ball with the back of another small paintbrush. Remove the ball from the paintbrush and set aside to dry.

GOLF TEE

1. Roll 20 g lime-green modelling paste into a sausage, tapering one end and forming a bulb at the other.
2. Push an extra-long toothpick through the centre of the paste, allowing 3 cm to protrude out of the tapered end.
3. Shape the bulb end into a golf tee head. Allow to dry.

ASSEMBLY

1. Brush the ganached cake with clear alcohol or lemon juice.
2. Roll out 1.2 kg light blue fondant to a thickness of 2 mm and cover the cake.
3. To create the argyle pattern on the cake, roll out 200 g black fondant to a thickness of 2 mm and cut out diamond shapes (see template on page 144). Glue the diamonds onto the sides of the cake with the tips of each shape touching. Cover the front first, followed by the sides and then the rear of the cake.
4. Dust the left half of each light blue space between the diamonds with deep blue dusting powder.
5. Fill a piping bag with white royal icing and fit a number 2 tube. Pipe diagonal lines across the diamonds, completing the argyle pattern.
6. Place the cake on the prepared cake board.
7. Stick the golf tee onto the top of the cake and attach the golf ball to the tee with a dot of white royal icing.
8. Fill an icing bag with lime-green royal icing and attach a grass tube. Pipe grass around the base of the cake and around the base of the golf tee.

Suppliers

A PIECE OF CAKE
All cake decorating supplies.
18 Upper High Street
Thame
Oxon OX9 3EX
www.apieceofcakethame.co.uk
Tel 0184 421 3428

ALDAVAL VEINERS (ALDV)
Suppliers of unique veiners such as cameo moulds.
16 Chibburn Court
Widdrington
Morpeth
Northumberland NE61 5QT
Tel 0167 079 0995

CAKE, CLASSES AND CUTTERS
*Offers cake decorating classes, makes celebration
cakes to order and supplies all cake decorating
equipment and ingredients.*
23 Princes Road
Brunton Park
Gosforth
Newcastle-upon-Tyne NE3 5TT
www.cakesclassesandcutters.co.uk
Tel 0191 217 0538

CAKE CRAFT SHOP
Supplies cake decorating equipment.
7 Chatterton Rd
Bromley
Kent BR2 9QW
www.cakecraftshop.co.uk
Tel 0173 246 3573

CELCAKES AND CELCRAFTS (CC)
*Suppliers of extensive range of cake decorating
equipment and tutorial DVDs and books.*
Springfield House
Gate Hemsley
York YO4 1NF
Tel 0175 937 2513
www.celcrafts.co.uk

CELEBRATIONS
*Supplies all cake decorating equipment and ingredients
and special occasion accessories as well as designing
and making novelty cakes to order.*
Unit 383 G
Jedburgh Court
Team Valley Trading Estate
Cateshead
Tyne and Wear NE11 0BQ
Tel 0191 487 7171
www.celebrations-teamvalley.co.uk

CORNELLI SUGARCRAFT SPECIALIST
Sugarcraft supplies and equipment.
1 Town Court High Street
Wendover
Bucks HP22 6EA
Tel 0129 669 6860
www.cornellisugarcraft.co.uk

CULPITT CAKE ART
*Suppliers of all baking and cake decorating equipment
and ingredients as well as special occasion accessories.*
Jubilee Industrial Estate
Ashington
Northumberland NE63 8UG
Tel 0167 081 5248
www.culpitt.com

DESIGN-A-CAKE
*Specialist sugarcraft equipment and ingredient supplier.
Also supplies other general baking supplies and
equipment such as cake stands for hire.*
30/31 Phoenix Road
Crowther Industrial Estate
Washington
Tyne and Wear NE38 0AD
Tel 0191 417 7377
www.design-a-cake.co.uk

GUY, PAUL AND CO LTD
UK distributor for Jem cutters. Suppliers of all sugarcraft and bakery supplies to trade.
Unit 10 The Business Centre
Corinium Industrial Estate
Raans Road
Amersham
Buckinghamshire HP6 6EB
Tel 0149 443 2121
www.guypaul.co.uk

HOLLY PRODUCTS (HP)
All cake decorating equipment and ingredients as well as tutorial DVDs and books.
Primrose Cottage
Church Walk
Norton in Hales
Shropshire TF9 4QX
Tel 0163 065 5759
www.hollyproducts.co.uk

ITEMS FOR SUGARCRAFT
Supplies all sugarcraft equipment and ingredients as well as decorated and unfinished celebration cakes.
72 Godstone Road
Kenley
Surrey CR8 5AA
Tel 0208 668 0251
www.itemsforsugarcraft.co.uk

JANE ASHER PARTY CAKES AND SUGARCRAFT
Online and retail supplier of cake decorating equipment and ingredients as well as special occasion accessories and cake decorating and cookery books.
22-24 Cale Street
London SW3 3QU
Tel: 0207 584 6177
www.jane-asher.co.uk

ORCHARD PRODUCTS (OPR)
Cake decorating equipment.
51 Hallyburton Road
Hove
East Sussex BN3 7GP
www.orchardcaketools.com
(temporarily closed at time of going to print)

PME
All cake decorating equipment.
Knightsbridge Bakeware Centre

Unit 23, Riverwalk Road
Enfield
Essex EN3 7QN
www.cakedecoration.co.uk

PRETTY WITTY CAKES
Online cake- and cupcake equipment and decorating supplier.
Rannoch Road
Crowborough
East Sussex TN6 1RB
Tel 079 7632 7278
www.prettywittycakes.co.uk

SQUIRES KITCHEN (SKHI)
Online and retail supplier of all things sugarcraft, equipment, ingredients, classes and books.
Squires House
3 Waverley Lane
Farnham
Surrey GU9 8BB
Tel 084 5617 1810
www.squires-shop.com

THE BRITISH SUGARCRAFT GUILD
National body that promotes the sugarcraft industry.
Wellington House
Messeter Place
Eltham
London SE9 5DP
www.bsguk.org

THE OLD BAKERY
Sugarcraft equipment specialising in stamens, Sunrise wires, Kingston pillars and Kingston cutters.
Kingston St Mary
Taunton
Somerset TA2 8HW
Tel 0182 345 1205
www.theoldbakery.co.uk

TINKERTECH TWO (TT)
Suppliers of cake decorating equipment.
40 Langdon Road
Parkstone
Poole
Dorset BH14 9EH
Tel 0120 273 8049

AUSTRALIA

BAKING PLEASURES
Online cake decorating equipment and ingredient suppliers.
www.bakingpleasures.com.au

CAKE DECO
Online and retail cake decorating equipment supplier.
Shop 7, Port Phillip Arcade
232 Flinders Street, Melbourne
Victoria, Australia
Tel 03 9654 5335
www.cakedeco.com.au

CAKES AROUND TOWN
All baking and cake decorating equipment and ingredients.
Unit 2/12 Sudbury Street
Darra
Brisbane QLD 4076
Tel 07 3160 8728
www.cakesaroundtown.com.au

COMPLETE CAKE DECORATING SUPPLIES
All cake decorating materials from tins to flower-making tools.

63 Boothby Street
Panorama
South Australia
5041
Tel 08 8299 0333
www.completecakedec.com.au

SOMETHING FOR CAKE
Online baking and cake decorating supplier.
10/202-204 Harbour Road
Brookvale NSW 2100
Australia
Tel 02 8084 4398
www.somethingforcake.com.au

THE SPOTTED APRON
All cake decorating materials from tins to flower-making tools.
Banksia Grove
Delamore Park
Perth WA
Tel: 04 14 157659
www.thespottedapron.com.au

NEW ZEALAND

CAKE STUFF
Cake decorating supplies and partyware.
322 Heretaunga Street
West Hastings
Tel 06 8703172
www.cakestuff.co.nz

MILLY'S KITCHEN SHOP – PARNELL
Has a specialised cake decorating department that includes equipment and ingredients.
Level 1
155 - 165 The Strand
Parnell
Tel 09 309 1690

MILLY'S KITCHEN SHOP – PONSONBY
Has a specialised cake decorating department that includes equipment and ingredients.

273 Ponsonby Road
Ponsonby
Auckland
Tel 09 376 1550

ROSEBOWL HOME COOKERY
A bakery, café, cake decorating equipment and ingredients supplier.
107 A Fergusson Street
Feilding
Tel 06 323 6765
www.rosebowl.co.nz

THE CAKE SHOP
Online cake decorating equipment and ingredients as well as DVDs and books supplier.
Tel 0800 222 454
www.thecakeshop.co.nz

WESTERN CAPE

CAB FOODS
Baking and decorating equipment and ingredients.
23 Kenwil Drive
Okavango Industrial Park
Brackenfell
Cape Town
7560
Tel 021 981 6778
www.cabfoods.co.za

CAKE CREATIONS
Sugarcraft equipment.
Corner 1st and Recreation Road
Fish Hoek
Cape Town
7975
Tel 021 782 8011
www.cakecreations.co.za

EBONY AND IVORY RIBBONS
Pettisham ribbons and trims.
52 Main Road
Diep River
7800
Cape Town
www.ebonyandivoryribbons.co.za

LET'S PARTY
Suppliers of baking and decorating equipment.
044 382 4384
Shop 2
Templeton Building
37 Main Road
Knysna
6570
www.letspartyknysna.co.za

VALUE BAKING SUPPLIES
Baking and decorating equipment and ingredients.
25 Tarentaal Crescent
Okavango Industrial
Brackenfell
7560
Cape Town
Tel 021 981 0304
www.valuebakingsupplies.co.za

THE BAKING TIN CLAREMONT
Baking and cake decorating equipment and ingredients.
Shop 52 Belvedere Road
Claremont
Cape Town
7708
Tel 021 671 6434
www.thebakingtin.co.za

THE BAKING TIN
Baking and cake decorating equipment and ingredients.
12 Harris Drive
Ottery East
Cape Town
7800
Tel 021 704 1710
www.thebakingtin.co.za

COUNTRYWIDE

SOUTH BAKELS (PTY) LTD
Suppliers of pettinice fondant and baking supplies.
www.sbakels.co.za

SPARKLEDUST
Online supplier of edible glitter.
www.sparkledust.co.za

GAUTENG

CHEFS 'N ICERS
Sugarcraft equipment.
Shop 3, Level 4
Sandton City
2146
Johanneburg
Tel 011 783 3201
www.chefs-n-icers.co.za

HERCULES BAKING SUPPLIES – BAKE-A-CAKE FRANCHISE
Suppliers of baking and decorating equipment and ingredients.
516 Karel Trichardt Avenue
Mountain View
Pretoria
0082
Tel 012 377 2668
www.bakeacake.co.za

THE CHOCOLATE DEN
Sugarcraft equipment and ingredients.
99 Linksfield Road
Glendower Shopping Centre
Edenvale
Johannesburg
2146
011 453-8160/7
www.chocolateden.co.za

THE SUGAR ART SHOP
Sugarcraft equipment.
140 10th Ave
Edenvale
Johannesburg
1609
Tel 011 452 3939
www.thesugarartshop.co.za

KWAZULU-NATAL

JEM CUTTERS
Flower and patchwork cutters.
128 Crompton Street
Pinetown
KwaZulu-Natal
3600
Tel 031 701 1431
www.jemcutters.com

FREE STATE

CHIPKINS BAKERY SUPPLIES (PTY) LTD
Suppliers of bulk baking ingredients and equipment.
28 Trannery Road
Hamilton
Bloemfontein
9301
Tel 051 435 3502
www.jemcutters.com

EASTERN CAPE

ALL THINGS CAKE
Supplies cake decorating ingredients.
Shop no 3
Balfour Park Shopping Centre
Balfour Road
Vincent
East London
5201
Tel 043 721 0697

Conversion chart

OVEN TEMPERATURES

	°C	°F	GAS MARK
very cool	100	200	¼
very cool	120	250	½
cool	150	300	2
moderate	160	325	3
moderate	180	350	4
moderate hot	190	375	5
hot	200	400	6
hot	220	425	7
very hot	240	475	9

CONVERSION TABLE

METRIC	IMPERIAL
Teaspoons	
2 ml	¼ tsp
3 ml	½ tsp
5 ml	1 tsp
10 ml	2 tsp
20 ml	4 tsp
TABLESPOONS	
15 ml	1 Tbsp
30 ml	2 Tbsp
45 ml	3 Tbsp
CUPS	
60 ml	¼ cup
80 ml	⅓ cup
125 ml	½ cup
160 ml	⅔ cup
200 ml	¾ cup
250 ml	1 cup
375 ml	1½ cups
500 ml	2 cups
1 litre	4 cups

Templates

fairy wings
(Tree stump cake – p. 52)

fairy princess wings
(Pillow cake and toadstool
cake – p. 108 and 128)

handbag flap
(Handbag cake – p. 68)

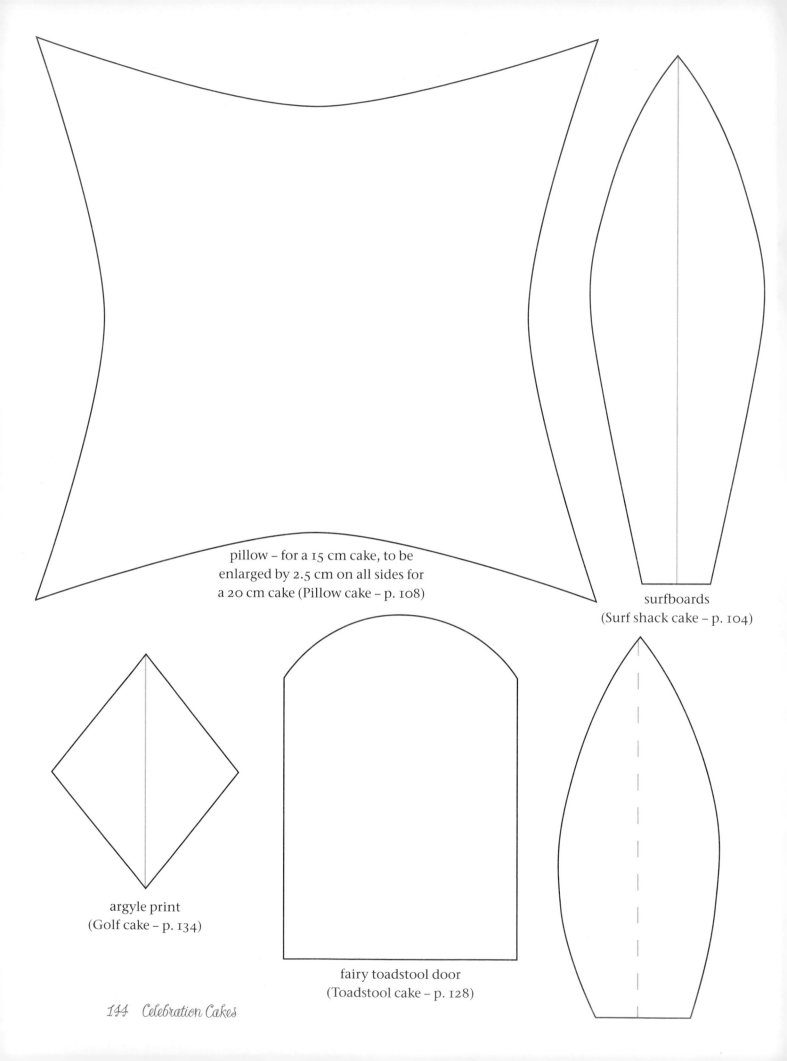

pillow – for a 15 cm cake, to be
enlarged by 2.5 cm on all sides for
a 20 cm cake (Pillow cake – p. 108)

surfboards
(Surf shack cake – p. 104)

argyle print
(Golf cake – p. 134)

fairy toadstool door
(Toadstool cake – p. 128)

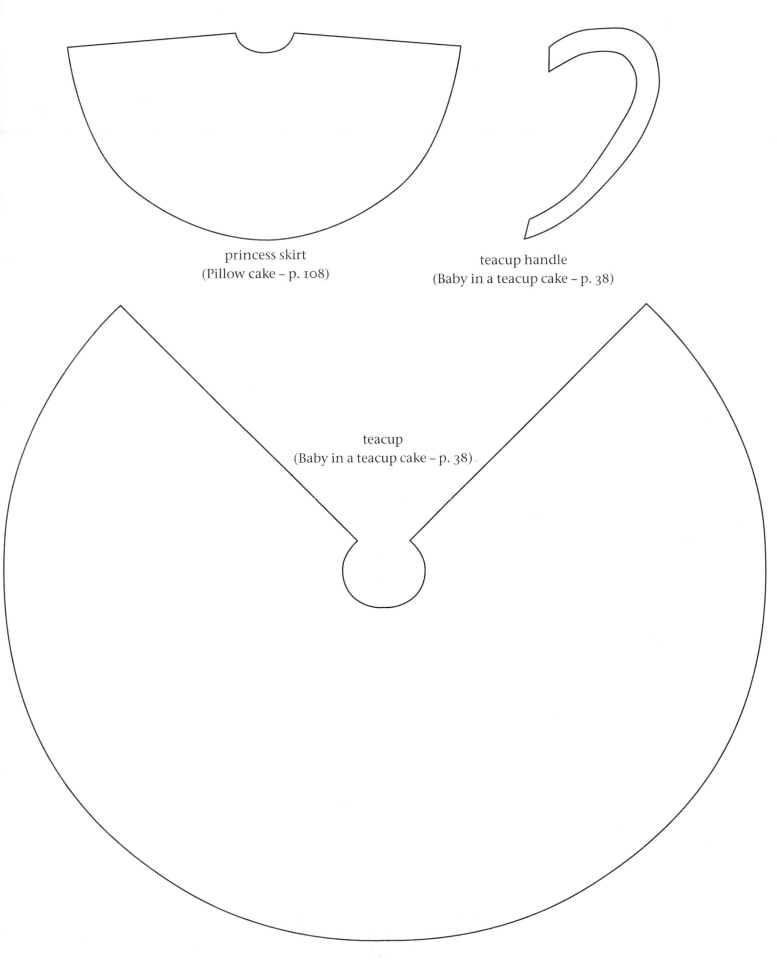

princess skirt
(Pillow cake – p. 108)

teacup handle
(Baby in a teacup cake – p. 38)

teacup
(Baby in a teacup cake – p. 38)

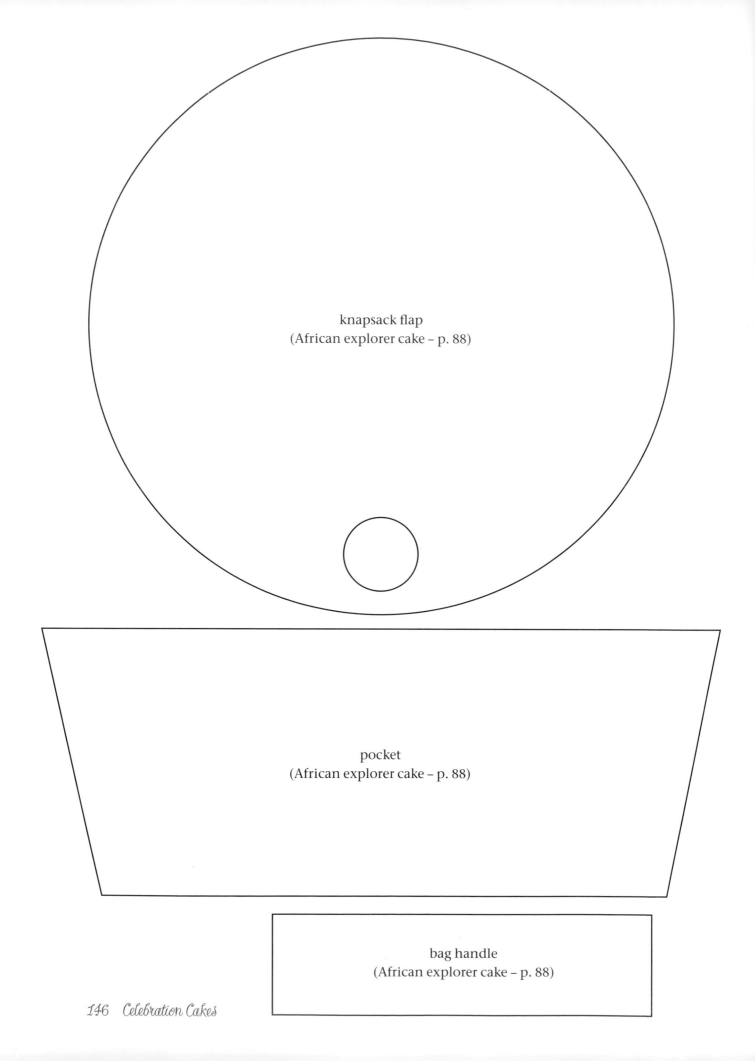

knapsack flap
(African explorer cake – p. 88)

pocket
(African explorer cake – p. 88)

bag handle
(African explorer cake – p. 88)

African explorer knapsack straps
(African explorer cake – p. 88)

handbag handle
(Handbag cake – p. 68)

straps must be 33 cm long
so this template must be double
this length

African explorer dragonfly wings
(African explorer cake – p. 88)

bag design shape (Handbag cake – p. 68)

Index

Acknowledgements

To the dedicated people at Struik Lifestyle for all the hard work and effort that went into putting this book together, including Monique for her creative talent.

To Warren Heath for the fabulous photos; you are a genius.

To my parents; you have grinned and eaten so many flops over the years.

To my sisters, Penny and Dot, who have shared many hours in the kitchen with me.

To my assistant, Wendy McLeod, for all the hours of help that you gave me with the cake preparation, typing and the million things that you did to make my job easier. Most of all for making me laugh when the dogs ate the cake.

To my children, Kellan, Julia-Anne and Simon, who are my inspiration, and to my late daughter, Sarah-Jane, who sparked my journey into sugar craft.

To my amazing friend, Kim, who never fails to amaze me; you are truly a breath of fresh air.

To my husband, Wayne; you are so encouraging and more supportive than I can ever repay.

To my students, you know who you are, who make sugar craft so much fun.

To CAB Foods for their kind donation of consumables.

To my heavenly father, this is a testimony to your faithfulness in my life.

Published in 2012 by Struik Lifestyle
(an imprint of Random House Struik (Pty) Ltd)
Company Reg. No 1966/003153/07
Wembley Square, Solan Road, Cape Town 8001
South Africa
PO Box 1144 Cape Town 8000 South Africa

www.randomstruik.co.za

Copyright © in published edition: Random House Struik (Pty) Ltd 2012
Copyright © in text: Grace Stevens 2012
Copyright © in photographs: Random House Struik (Pty) Ltd 2012

ISBN 978-143170-208-4 (Print)
ISBN 978-143230-146-0 (e-Pub)
ISBN 978-143230-147-7 (PDF)

PUBLISHER: Linda de Villiers
MANAGING EDITOR: Cecilia Barfield
DESIGN MANAGER: Beverley Dodd
EDITORS: Bronwen Leak, Anja Grobler
DESIGNER: Monique Oberholzer
PHOTOGRAPHER: Warren Heath
PROOFREADER: Laetitia Sullivan
INDEXER: Anja Grobler

Reproduction by Hirt & Carter Cape (Pty) Ltd
Printing and binding by Craft Print International Pte Ltd, Singapore